# THE BUTTERFLY GARDEN

*Buddleia, or butterfly bush, here attracting the Red Admiral (left) and Cabbage White (right).*

# T H E
# BUTTERFLY
# GARDEN

## MATHEW TEKULSKY

*Illustrated by Susanah Brown*

*Introduction by Robert Michael Pyle*

THE HARVARD COMMON PRESS

*Harvard and Boston, Massachusetts*

The Harvard Common Press
535 Albany Street
Boston, Massachusetts 02118

*Printed in the United States of America.*

LIBRARY OF CONGRESS CATALOGING IN PUBLICATION DATA
Tekulsky, Mathew, 1954–
The butterfly garden.

Bibliography: p.
Includes index.
1. Butterflies.   2. Wildlife attracting.   3. Gardening.   I. Title.
QL544.T45        1985        638'.5789          85-8609
ISBN 0-916782-70-0
ISBN 0-916782-69-7 (pbk.)

*Book design by Joyce Weston*
*Cover art by Susanah Brown*

*10  9*

# CONTENTS

# ACKNOWLEDGEMENTS

I would like to express my appreciation to the many people who were so generous with their time and expertise. In particular, I would like to thank Robert Michael Pyle for his technical and editorial advice and encouragement; Jane Jordan Browne, my literary agent, and Bruce Shaw, of The Harvard Common Press, for believing in this book; Linda Ziedrich, Scott McEathron, and especially Anne Vilen, for their editorial contributions; Leslie Baker and Joyce Weston, for their production work; and Susanah Brown, for her illustrations. For their technical assistance, I would like to thank Julian Donahue, John Emmel, John Garth, Charles Hogue, Steven Kutcher, Tony Leigh, Rudi Mattoni, and Everett Olson. I would also like to thank Linda Hardie-Scott, for her help regarding wildflowers. Thanks as well to the Lorquin Entomological Society in Los Angeles.

*To my parents,*
*who first instilled in me an appreciation for and love of nature.*

# THE BUTTERFLY
# GARDEN

# INTRODUCTION

*Robert Michael Pyle*

As a young boy, I developed a passion for seashells and land snails. My obsession was doomed to be frustrated, on account of my habitat. The plains east of Denver, Colorado, offered little hope of gratification for the young conchologist. My hobby handbook insisted that "snails frequent damp gardens." So, sustained by treasures from the Denver Museum of Natural History gift shop and fixes from the "Shell of the Month Club," I prowled the raw new gardens of suburbia after every thundershower. Not a snail revealed itself to my prying eyes and muddy fingers.

Many a young would-be naturalist has probably died a death from such withheld gratification. Fortunately, those garden-prowls turned up other finds that, in time, turned my eye toward a more rewarding resource for a Colorado lad. For I found cocoons of moths and beetle pupae, earwigs and sowbugs and caterpillars. These items were not without their own charm and interest to my eyes. About the same time I began to notice butterflies and moths coming to the flowers my mother had so lovingly nourished on the bare, bulldozed ground of the post-plains home-site. Returning to my young collector's handbook, I learned the amazing fact that such winged visions came from the very kinds of creatures I'd been discovering on leaf and under stone.

Naturally, I became an insect collector. I lost the chase to Mourning Cloaks, stuffed unfortunate Painted Ladies in makeshift containers without a clue how to kill them, impaled sphinx moths on common pins as I held chloroform to their nostril-less "noses." In time my techniques improved, and I went farther afield. But I never left my garden entirely, for as it matured, more and more different kinds of butterflies showed up in my own backyard. Tawny Skippers and Tailed Blues dallied over the clover. Mourning Cloaks and Weidemeyer's Admirals, grand animals that they were and still are to me, each claimed boughs of our weeping willow from which to patrol territories only they could see. A male Hackberry Butterfly returned each summer (not the same one, I finally figured out) to reclaim such a post on a Chinese elm, in spite of the fact that the nearest hackberry tree stood a full block away. And most desired, Tiger Swallowtails drank draughts from the lilacs that intoxicated me as well, just as they did in a painting from a treasured article in an old *National Geographic*.

Those lilacs! Without knowing it, my mother practiced butterfly gardening for her future lepidopterist when she planted them. Black Swallowtails, Satyr Anglewings, and White-lined Sphinx Moths also loved their nectar. But their greatest utility came when I first attempted to rear Cecropia Moths from a vial of eggs I'd bought. Having read they would eat lilac leaves, I began feeding the young larvae individually in their test tubes; then, *en masse* in a laundry tub. But they required so many leaves, so often, and produced so much frass that needed cleaning out, that in desperation I finally dumped the whole lot—about 200 fingerling larvae, each ravenous—onto the lilac bushes themselves. In a fortnight they had become great green serpents, blue-and-red-bumped and the size of a coal-miner's thumb. Although far fewer survived to make their huge cocoons, they did so at the dear expense of those poor lilacs. The nearly defoliated bushes barely survived the ordeal, and my insect gardening continued only by dint of a highly indulgent, nature-loving mother. Quite possibly, the origin of the East Denver Cecropia Moth population dates from that debacle.

Other gardens, other memories. When I worked with my grandmother in her rich, mature mid-Denver garden, I remained ever alert for the vast shadow that meant a Two-tailed Tiger Swallowtail sailing in to rob the sweet rockets' nectar. My mother and I would prowl the parkways of the neighborhood, watching and sometimes catching colorful forester moths and day-flying hawkmoths on great patches of phlox and rocket. We often took things home to rear, and we began planting special seeds for the host plants and nectar lures they would yield.

I noticed that other yards on the block offered species that seldom called at my house. To find Hackberry Butterfly larvae and pupae, bright green booty respectively tailed and serrated, I had to visit the hackberry trees down the block. Painted Ladies dawdled briefly at our zinnias but really hung out at the butterfly bushes three houses away. How I coveted those buddleias, and what a pest I must have been to their owners. Even today the purple pungency of a butterfly bush recalls the sweet intensity of the pre-adolescent chase, when butterflies were all.

Through all the distractions and vicissitudes of the quarter-century since, butterflies have remained a mainmast of mine. I have been fortunate to watch butterflies from the Highlands of Scotland to the Highlands of New Guinea, from the Monarch forests of Mexico to the rainforests of Costa Rica, and across much of North America. And still, gardens play a major role in my butterfly-life. Wherever I travel, I head for botanical gardens. I had some of my best Russian butterfly watching in the botanical garden of Turkmenia in Ashkhabad. Likewise, as a houseguest I am likely to spend more time in my hosts' gardens than their homes. I will never forget a brief convalescence in Hong Kong, when my fever was beautifully cooled by a tropic rain and the Paris Swallowtail that nectared by my garden window in the fresh air of its aftermath. A few days later, I finally photographed the tailed maroon satyr I'd been seeking—in a formal Chinese garden.

Now I have a home of my own and travel less. Sunny summer days in western Washington being rather rare and precious, it is especially important to me to have an immediate environment where I can dash outside and catch the sunshine—and watch butterflies—whenever the clouds choose to part. I reside, perhaps, in one of the poorest parts of the country for butterfly abundance and diversity. Yet this fact hardly matters when the Western Tiger and Pale Tiger Swallowtails weigh down the rhododendrons, ruby-spotted Clodius Parnassians flock to the bramble blossoms, and Woodland Skippers shoot between the asters like nuggets from a slingshot. These and others I can encourage by the plantings I choose to make and the ways in which I decide to manage the inexorable growth of green that colors the Maritime Northwest.

It is important for all would-be butterfly gardeners to realize that *gardening is a form of land management.* We might like to manage the bits of land that are "ours" to care for through benign neglect: a bit of butterfly weed here, a carrot patch over there, a milkweed pod crushed and cast to the wind—and the rest all left to time, rain, and nature. If I did that, my old Swedish homestead with its century-old oaks and odd hybrid

3

ecosystem would be so quickly engulfed in brambles and coarse grasses that scarcely a path could be walked or a butterfly spotted. The parnassians' bleeding heart would wither from the competition, the heath and wild pea-patch where I hope to establish Silvery Blues and Brown Elfins would disappear. The least possible interference may well be the best, in some cases and places. But for most gardens, management decisions make them what they are, or are capable of becoming. In its planning and execution, management provides much of the challenge of this odd but joyful enterprise we call butterfly gardening.

If you are lucky enough to own a piece of undisturbed wildland, by all means keep it that way. The native species will not benefit from your ministrations to any great extent. But most of us occupy city lots, suburban plats, or rural realms of weeds and wildflowers mixed so as to resemble the native landscape little or not at all. To all these brands of cultivated countryside, we can bring a measure of butterfly numbers and kinds that would not otherwise exist—through appropriate garden management, aimed at the specific needs of these delicate visitors. It is not necessarily easy (although it may be relaxed) and it can become a lot of hard work. But if we are diligent, we may attract quite a few species; and if we are clever or lucky, we may even induce the courted creatures to remain. The satisfactions are immense.

What we have lacked, until now, was a comprehensive handbook to the practice of butterfly gardening. A flock of magazine articles, a handful of pamphlets, and a short shelf of British books introduced the subject and beguiled many with the bright possibilities of wooing butterflies to their very doorstep. But with our vast national passion for gardening and our primitive awareness of butterflies, we needed a peculiarly North American approach to the subject.

Mathew Tekulsky has filled the gap with this excellent book. Taking the broad view from Maine to Malibu, Miami to my own Northwest, he has created a text of great usefulness. Matt assumes that you know little about butterflies to begin with, insures that you will know quite a lot when you finish. With thoroughness and a zeal born of personal love for the butterflies themselves, he takes us through the process of building a butterfly garden, from scratch. Explaining all the necessary steps in a clear, interpretive style, he leaves plenty of room for the creative imagination of each reader/gardener/butterfly lover. I, for one, wish I had owned such a book long ago.

4

INTRODUCTION

Whether you come to this book as a butterfly person or a plant person or neither, you will forever after be both. And as a butterfly gardener, your life will never be quite the same. The power to enrich a patch of Earth with beautiful butterflies, no matter how humble the plot or simple the effort, is awesome. And the Earth needs this kind of power.

As the author explains, butterflies have had some hard times lately. Whatever we can do as individuals to help stanch the wounds a careless society inflicts on the land, we must do. Butterfly gardening is such an act. It will never replace the setting aside of nature reserves for the preservation of natural diversity, but it can help. Perhaps most importantly, it keeps people in touch with nature on an everyday, first-name basis; and that in itself can only lead to better, more sensitive Earth stewardship on the part of the people as a whole.

Whether you really go to town with your butterfly garden or settle for modest efforts and expectations, develop and engineer a master plan for acres, or blow a milkweed pod over your backyard and lie back in the hammock to see what happens, you will have fun. That is the most important message in Mr. Tekulsky's book. Butterflies mean fun and deep pleasure, and butterfly gardening gives you a means of finding them. Along with valuable lists of nectar and host plants, supply sources, helpful groups, and literature both instructive and inspirational, Mathew Tekulsky has written an entertaining account of getting to know the insects in question. He gives us activities for their enjoyment, tips for their rearing, and much of what we need to know to bring home the butterflies. The rest is up to us.

There is no such thing as a typical butterfly garden, or gardener. For one person the ideal might be a window box full of zinnias and everlasting, supporting a colony of West Coast Ladies. For another, an average suburban yard planted with forage and nectar for a score of species. Farmers may wish to manage their marginal lands for all wildlife, including butterflies. Still other people construct butterfly greenhouses, great or small, where tropical species carry out their life cycles in full view. Clearly, you may suit yourself as you seek to suit butterflies. Imagination and the insects themselves provide the only limits to ambition. As in nature herself, *vive la différence*.

The chief traits all butterfly gardeners have in common are the desire and design to provide for the needs of butterflies, however briefly, and thus to attract them. Winston Churchill did it with Peacock butterflies and nettlebeds, much to the consternation of his head gardener. Edwin Way Teale did it with an old orchard, for which he leased the "insect rights." Roger Tory Peterson does it with black-eyed Susans and Great Spangled Fritillaries. And thousands of ordinary nature lovers do it with butterfly bush and butterfly weed, carrots and phlox, monarchs and swallowtails, to their everlasting joy and satisfaction. Shouldn't you do it too?

R.M.P.

# WHAT IS BUTTERFLY GARDENING?

You are standing deep in meadow wildflowers, beneath a bright, sun-filled sky. A whisper of breeze tussles the fireweed, bleeding hearts, thistles, and black-eyed Susans around you. Suddenly your eye catches a Monarch butterfly, royally adorned in its brilliant orange and black velvet, lifting itself skyward from a throne of daisies. It flutters, teeters crazily in a sudden down-current of air and settles gently onto the ball-shaped white head of a buttonbush. Despite your attentive gaze, it goes on with its business sipping through its proboscis at the scores of tiny white blossoms. Then this most enchanting of insects withdraws, lifts its fragile wings, and disappears over a distant bed of lavender.

Throughout history, man has watched the ethereal flight of butterflies with awe and wonder. Butterflies have been the inspiration of poets and the solace of pouting children. In recent times, entomologists, both professional and amateur, have studied, and remarked on the adaptability of butterfies to environments radically changed by man. Today, that adaptability is being taken advantage of by a new breed of observers—butterfly gardeners. Whether a suburban resident, owner of a small urban garden plot, apartment dweller, or keeper of a country estate, you can enjoy frequent butterfly visits to your garden or window box. All you need to get started is a basic knowledge of butterfly characteristics and behavior and a desire to learn the specific needs and habits of butterfly species which are common in your neighborhood.

The greatest inspiration and incentive to become a dedicated butterfly gardener will probably arrive with your first flock of friendly fritillaries or the uninvited compliment of a solitary Mourning Cloak settling onto your shoulder. Spurred on by these firsthand encounters with the mysterious butterfly world, you may decide to expand your efforts to include what Dr. Herbert Kulman, an entomolgist at the University of Minnesota, calls "butterfly production management," the manipulation of butterfly habitats to insure a maximum number and diversity of butterflies in a selected area. By cultivating the specific food plants of selected butterfly species and providing propitious conditions for egg laying, caterpillar survival, and metamorphosis, you can actually regulate what kinds and how many butterflies attend your garden.

Perhaps most satisfying, you might help insure the continued and increased prosperity of common butterflies that are threatened by the destruction of their wild habitats. Since most rare butterfly species do not inhabit gardens, it may be an exaggeration to suggest that gardens can play a primary role in preserving the diversity of species found in the wild. Still, your efforts on behalf of butterflies generally may help educate your neighbors to the preservation needs of endangered species of Lepidoptera. And, as British biologist Dr. Denis Owen has noted, surburbia, with its rich diversity of native and exotic plants supporting "an almost incredible variety" of insect species, is expanding, and likewise its responsibility to accommodate and preserve the creatures which inhabit it.

## BUTTERFLY CLASSIFICATION

In preparation for butterfly gardening, you will need to learn which of the nearly seven hundred species in North America north of Mexico are indigenous to your area, which are most plentiful and easiest to attract, and what flowers and vegetation they nectar and lay eggs on. A basic lesson in butterfly classification is a helpful beginning.

The fifty common garden butterflies listed in the appendix, and most other butterflies as well, fall into seven general families based on coloration, shape, and other characteristics. **Brush-footed butterflies,** or nymphalids, comprise butterflies which have stunted front legs that barely reach the ends of their bodies. About one third of all North American species, including the commonly sighted Viceroy and Mourning Cloak, fall into this category. **Gossamer wings** include many small brown and blue butterflies like the Silvery Blue and Brown Elfin. The

**milkweed butterflies'** most prominent member is the well-known Monarch. **Satyr or brown butterflies** frequently rest on tree trunks where they are disguised from predators. **Skippers**, like the Tawny-edged Skipper, look like miniature fighter planes or small dark butterfly miniatures that dart or skip about close to the ground. **Swallowtails** have a tail on the end of each wing, and the Two-tailed and Three-tailed Tiger Swallowtails—as their names imply—have more than one. Finally, **whites** or **sulphurs**, are white or yellow in color and include such common members as the Cabbage White (or Cabbage Butterfly).

Butterflies can be further distinguished by wing pattern. Hairstreaks have streaky lines on their underwings and usually have one or two thin tails extending from each hindwing. Checkerspots have irregular, checkered patterns of black, brown, orange, yellow, and white on their wings. Crescentspots have pearly or silvery chevrons on their underwings. Longwings have narrow, curved wings with a wide span. Lastly, anglewings have jagged angular wings. Two anglewings, the Comma and the Question Mark, are aptly named for the peculiar markings which punctuate the undersides of their hindwings.

*The Cabbage White caterpillar feeding on common nasturtium, one of its favorite food plants. An adult hovers nearby.*

9

Less conspicuous characteristics like eye color and antenna shape also distinguish butterfly species from each other and from their co-members of the Order Lepidoptera (derived from the Greek *lepis*, scale, and *ptera*, wing)—the moths. These differences will be described in Chapter Two.

It is also important to know that while some species of butterflies, most notably the Monarch, migrate through many regions of this country, or move north temporarily during the warm seasons, others live out their entire lives within a single region and will rarely be seen elsewhere. Which butterflies are most common in your region will be addressed in Chapter Three. For further information on the numerous plant and butterfly species used as examples in this text, refer to the appendix.

## THE LIFE CYCLE OF YOUR GARDEN

In order to design a successful butterfly garden, you will also need to know something about the butterfly life cycles. The butterflies we typically think of are adult butterflies, which spend their days sipping flower nectar through tube-like proboscises which they uncoil from under their heads. To bring these adult butterflies into your garden, you will need to plant the nectar sources and food plants which are frequented by the various species in your neighborhood.

Although some butterfly species are attracted to a wide range of nectar sources, others express definite preferences in size, shape, or color of flowers. The Eastern Tailed Blue, a small butterfly with a short proboscis, for instance, finds short-tubed or open flowers like clover, cinquefoil, and fleabane most tasty, according to Dr. Paul Opler, author of *Butterflies East of the Great Plains*. What motivates these preferences and how you can employ them to your garden's advantage will be addressed in a later section of this book.

Having attracted adult butterflies to your garden, you can prolong their stay by encouraging them to mate and lay eggs in your garden. Female butterflies are much more selective of the plants on which they lay eggs than they are of nectar plants, because only certain species-specific plants contain the chemical constituents needed to nurture their caterpillars.

In a 1967 *Scientific American* article, Drs. Paul Ehrlich and Peter Raven contend that this phenomenon can be explained by the coevolution of plants and their insect predators. Over the millennia, plants have evolved chemicals that repel most insects. However, some caterpillars have become so adapted to cope with the substances of their particular hosts that they have actually come to require them in their diets. Hence, different species of butterflies have minimized their competition with each other and other insects by developing tolerances for feeding only on certain larval food plants. The larvae of some whites, for example, feed primarily on the plants of the mustard and caper families, which contain oils that repel other herbivorous insects.

The specialization of various species of larvae illustrates the intimate interaction between the plant world and the butterfly world. Samuel Hubbard Scudder, a nineteenth-century botanist, wrote in his classic work *Frail Children of the Air*, "In many, perhaps the majority of instances, the plants upon which allied species or genera of caterpillars feed, themselves belong to allied families of the botanical system." Almost a century later, Ehrlich and Raven, working on the same principle, have suggested that the citrus and parsley families, although previously not considered related, may actually have much in common because various swallowtail caterpillars feed on the essential oils present in both the citrus and parsley families of plants.

To encourage the butterfly species which live in your garden to remain throughout their life cycle, therefore, you will have to know which host plants they prefer. Frequently these plants are also human food plants, in other words, vegetables. So, you may need to plant an extra allotment to satisfy both your culinary and entomological tastes.

Jo Brewer, a Massachusetts butterfly gardener, reports that she shares her parsley with Black Swallowtail larvae, which also enjoy other wild and cultivated members of the carrot family. California entomologist Steven Kutcher harvests fennel for his salads, but leaves a generous helping for his garden's Anise Swallowtails. He also raises radishes and broccoli for the Cabbage Butterfly and shares his tomato plants with the larvae of the Five-spotted Sphinx Moth, less solicitously dubbed the tomato hornworm.

An avid vegetable gardener's concern about caterpillar infestation is understandable, but usually unwarranted, since the predators and parasites which co-exist with caterpillars in a natural garden usually keep them under control. Spiders, wasps, ants, flies, and beetles join forces with birds, small mammals, and inclement weather against caterpillars

*11*

*The Spicebush Swallowtail expresses a fondness for Japanese honeysuckle.*

to protect plants from irreparable damage and insure the prosperity of your garden as well as your butterflies.

In one study, butterflies were even found to regulate their own population. In the autumn of 1963, V.G. Dethier and Robert MacArthur placed an additional 19,800 Harris' Checkerspot caterpillars into a field already containing a modest 800 or so larvae. A year later, the larval population had fallen to 400, which, the scientists claimed, was "about what it would have been had there been no new larvae introduced." Having also observed the adult females' newfound liking for a nearby patch of asters, Dethier and MacArthur concluded that the females had laid far fewer eggs in the field after the artificial infestation, in order to insure an adequate food supply for their larvae.

If the caterpillar overpopulation does become a problem in your

*12*

garden, the larvae can be gathered and transferred to a plant of the same kind some distance from your yard or to a wild plant. Careful spraying is condoned in extreme cases but discouraged, since pesticides kill not only butterfly larvae but their predators, thereby altering the tenuous balance of nature. Also, it is instructive to remember that some butterflies contribute greatly to weed control. During mass migrations, Monarchs devour millions of milkweed plants. Painted Ladies cut back wide areas of thistles. And the Red Admiral, Comma, Satyr Anglewing, and Milbert's Tortoiseshell consume countless patches of stinging nettles each year. The Fiery Skipper may even trim your Bermuda grass for you.

When a caterpillar becomes full-grown, it pupates and begins its magical transformation, or metamorphosis, into an adult butterfly. When it emerges, days or even months later, you will want to have its favorite nectar sources available. You may even consider building a butterfly house or cage, complete with the proper food plants, in which the silent chrysalises can develop and open before your eyes. A detailed explanation of how to build and care for such containers will be given in Chapter Eight.

## THE FIRST STEP

Undoubtedly the most challenging initial step of starting a butterfly garden is learning which species of butterflies it is possible to attract to your garden and what nectar sources and food plants these species like. Begin, with the help of a good indentification field guide, by conducting a local survey of common butterflies in your neighborhood. Visit local fields, forests, and parks, as well as gardens; jot down which kinds of flowers you see the butterflies feeding on. Certain species and flowers are more plentiful during one season than another, so make your observations throughout the year.

Don't be deterred by the apparent scarcity of butterflies in urban areas or by the fact that you live in an apartment building. Many wild plants which attract butterflies to rural areas can be transplanted into or cultivated from purchased seed in city gardens. As an apartment dweller, I have reared several different species of butterflies, including Gulf Fritillaries, Monarchs, and Anise Swallowtails. And without leaving my urban neighborhood, I have observed a colony of Gray Hairstreaks enjoying a boulevard hibiscus, Fiery Skippers playing in the lawn, Cabbage Butterflies laying their eggs on nearby nasturtiums, Mourning Cloaks bedding down in the streetside elms, and occasionally a Checkered White, Sleepy Orange, or Western Tiger Swallowtail nectaring on coreopsis, sweet alyssum, or geraniums.

Remember too, butterfly populations and ranges can fluctuate from year to year and are constantly influenced by changing environmental factors and, seemingly, by the charming but fickle whim of the butterflies. Common Sulphurs may fill up your garden one year and be hardly visible the next. Indeed, you may think the world has run out of Silvery Blues, only to discover that the fellow down the street has a whole colony of them in his garden. Nevertheless, over several seasons, as your knowledge and insight increase, you will learn to manipulate the environment of your garden to suit the butterflies in your area and will spend more and more hours reaping the aesthetic pleasures of butterflies on the wing.

## ENTHUSIASTS TO EMULATE

As inspiration, consider the centuries of butterfly gardeners who have preceded you. Among the people whose encounters with butterflies have changed their lives, were Californian Charles McGlashan and his daughter Ximena, who started a butterfly farm for profit and wound up publishing *The Butterfly Farmer: A Monthly Magazine for Amateur Entomologists*. Following this pair's example, Albert and Amy Carter, during the 1930's, ran a small, screened-in public park populated by 16,000 home-grown butterflies.

Perhaps the first historical luminary to express his fascination with butterflies was the Greek philosopher Aristotle, who described the life cycle of the Cabbage Butterfly. Several centuries later, Sir Winston Churchill began a butterfly garden at his Chartwell estate in Kent, England. For several years, the estate was repeatedly stocked with more than a thousand butterflies—to the great delight of the enamored Churchill, who even went so far as to convert a summerhouse into a butterfly house for raising caterpillars and chrysalises.

The late Soviet émigré novelist Vladimir Nabokov was another butterfly enthusiast, whose eloquence and insight on these fragile, winged creatures is unequaled. In his autobiography, *Speak, Memory*, Nabokov

*The Mourning Cloak, pictured here on an elm, uses this and other trees as food plants.*

recalls the dreamlike butterfly experiences in the garden of his family's summer home near St. Petersburg.

> From the age of seven, everything I felt in connection with a rectangle of framed sunlight was dominated by a single passion. If my first glance of the morning was for the sun, my first thought was for the butterflies it would engender. . . . On the honeysuckle, overhanging the carved back of a bench just opposite the main entrance, my guiding angel . . . pointed out to me a rare visitor, a splendid, pale-yellow creature with black blotches, blue crenels, and a cinnabar eyespot above each chrome-rimmed black tail. As it probed the inclined flower from which it hung, its powdery body slightly bent, it kept restlessly jerking its great wings, and my desire for it was one of the most intense I have ever experienced.

Nabokov later became a renowed lepidopterist and named, among other butterflies, the Karner Blue (a subspecies of the Orange-bordered Blue), which exists in various parts of the northern Midwest and Northeast and is a protected insect in New York State. After that, he continued

*15*

to write passionately and inspirationally about the charmed existence of butterflies and the enchantment of those who watch them.

> I confess I do not believe in time. . . . And the highest enjoyment of timelessness . . . is when I stand among rare butterflies and their food plants. This is ecstasy, and behind the ecstasy is something else, which is hard to explain. It is like a momentary vacuum into which rushes all that I love. A sense of oneness with sun and stone. A thrill of gratitude to whom it may concern—to the contrapuntal genius of human fate or to tender ghosts humoring a lucky mortal.

# BUTTERFLY LIVES

The array of markings, shapes, sizes, colors, and lesser characteristics displayed by the fifteen to twenty thousand species of butterflies worldwide is truly mind boggling. But what is perhaps more surprising is that often these qualities differ even between males and females or successive generations of a single species. They can also be used to positively identify species which differ only in a single minute characteristic or to recognize at a glance remarkably distinctive butterfly species as well as the butterflies' relatives, the moths.

## VARIETY AND DIVERSITY

Males and females in many butterfly species appear markedly different. Blue males usually have bright-blue wings, whereas females are often brown or gray, a feature which allows them to camouflage themselves more easily during egg laying. The male Eastern Black Swallowtail is yellow and black, but the female mimics the black and blue coloration of the Pipevine Swallowtail. While northern female Tiger Swallowtails are yellow and black like their mates, a large portion of those in the South are dark, appearing again, much like the Pipevine Swallowtail.

The successive generations of some species, hatched in different seasons, may also contrast in appearance. The summer generations of the Comma and Question Mark have dark hindwings, while the fall generation's hindwings are orange. The spring generation of the Zebra Swallowtail is smaller, paler, and has tails half as long as its offspring hatched in summer. Variation between broods has to do with seasonal changes in atmospheric conditions. Geographic variations, on the other hand, may be determined either environmentally or genetically. The Viceroy, for instance, mimics the Monarch's coloration in most of its range but in the Deep South it has adapted to resemble the darker, mahogany-brown Queen.

The unique coloration of some butterflies defies categorization and enables even the least observant butterfly enthusiast to recognize them at a moment's glance. The Buckeye, with its shiny, bluish-purple eyespots set against a tawny-brown background, is easily identified nectaring among the asters. The orange-red bars glistening on the black garments of the Red Admiral earn this butterfly its prestigious name. And the Mourning Cloak wears its mahogany cape decorated with a creamy, yellow border and bluish-violet spots as gracefully as the finest nobleman.

Though less conspicuous than coloration, markings, or wing shape, the texture and color of the proboscis, eye color, and body structure also differ between individual butterfly species, and between butterflies and moths. The proboscis of the Gulf Fritillary, for example, is light-brown in color, while the Anise Swallowtail's is shiny and black like shoestring licorice. The latter's eyes are also black, in contrast to the Gulf Fritillary's orange eyes and the Cabbage Butterfly's light-green ones.

The body structure of moths differs markedly from that of butterflies. While both butterflies and moths have scaly wings, butterflies have clubbed antennae with a swelling at the tip, and moths have slim or feathery antennae which taper to a fine point. The bodies of most butterflies are slender and bare, while moth bodies are often thick and hairy. When at rest, butterflies hold their wings upright over their backs; moths tend to hold them out flat. Butterflies fly during the day; most moths fly at night. Except for the skippers, most butterflies pupate in naked chrysalises, while most moths spin cocoons in which their pupae develop. Since there are at least ten times as many moth species as butterflies, you may also want to invite moths to your garden.

The butterfly kingdom can be observed in astounding variety and diversity within a single small area of vegetation. In 1955, William H. Howe, author of *The Butterflies of North America*, collected sixty-four butterfly species on his nine-acre farm in Ottawa, Kansas, and an additional eighteen species within a mile of the property. Thirty-one of the species he found are included in the "Fifty Common Garden Butterflies" section at the back of this book—including the Monarch, Mourning Cloak, Painted Lady, Buckeye, Red-spotted Purple, and Tiger Swallowtail.

## THE LIFE CYCLE

Butterflies go through four distinct stages in their life cycle: egg, or ovum (plural, ova); caterpillar, or larva (plural larvae); chrysalis, or pupa (plural pupae); adult, or imago (plural imagoes). Each butterfly species has a distinctive appearance in each stage. In fact, it is often possible to identify a species from its immature forms. Some field guides have illustrations of caterpillars, chrysalises, and even eggs, but when illustrations aren't available, observation in your garden or rearing butterflies will help you identify the young of various species.

## THE EGG

The coloration and shape of butterfly eggs foreshadows the rainbow of adult appearances. The Gulf Fritillary's eggs when just laid are lightyellow, oblong, and marked by longitudinal striations. The Tiger Swallowtail's are yellow-green and spherical. Note too that the eggs of most species change as the caterpillars inside them mature. The Gulf Fritillary's eggs turn amber after a day and remain dark until they hatch. And the keg-shaped eggs of the Mourning Cloak change from pale to black as they develop. The majority of eggs are less than a millimeter in diameter and hatch within a week after being deposited. In some species, however, eggs are able to withstand the harshness of winter and lie dormant for as long as two years before hatching.

## THE CATERPILLAR

Caterpillars are built primarily for eating. Their large heads have hard shells, or capsules around them. Each side of the head features a group of simple eyes, or ocelli. A pair of antennae extend from the front of the head. Below the antennae is a silk spinneret (on the lower "lip") and a pair of mandibles for chewing. A caterpillar's first three pairs of legs (the "true" legs) are jointed, and each has a little claw at the end.

19

*Different butterfly families are here represented by the Dogface butterfly, Silvery Blue, Milbert's Tortoiseshell, Giant Swallowtail, Fiery Skipper, Eyed Brown, and Queen.*

Farther down on its body are five pairs of prolegs, which it uses for gripping. The last pair, called the anal prolegs, are separated from the others by a wide gap.

Although caterpillars are structurally alike, different species exhibit differences in size, shape, and color. The Common Blue caterpillar, for instance, has a sluglike green body covered with short white hairs and is about three-eighths of an inch long. Black spines bristle from the one-inch-long body of the black and orange Baltimore. And the Black Swallowtail larva has a black band with yellow or orange spots on each segment of its two-inch-long green body.

A caterpillar's life is dominated by feeding, first usually on its egg-shell, and then on the tender leaves or flowers of its host plant. Once its mouth parts have hardened, a caterpillar is able to chew and consume nearly any part of its food plant, including stems. Each species also displays a distinctive feeding pattern, and where there are a great many individuals of one species, that plant may suffer considerable damage.

Seemingly vulnerable creatures, caterpillars have evolved ingenious ways to protect themselves from their many predators. Some species feed primarily at night. Those which feed during the day commonly camouflage themselves upon their food plants. The Cabbage Butterfly, for

instance, adopts different shades of green depending on whether it is feeding on dark green nasturtium or pale green cabbage. Caterpillars also tend to feed on the underside of leaves, which keeps them invisible to aerial predators and shields them from the drying effects of the sun. Spines or hairs sported by many caterpillars dissuade predators. Other species, like the larvae of the Monarch, feed on poisonous plants which make them distasteful to predators. Swallowtail larvae project two-pronged, light-orange fleshy organs called osmeteria (singular osmeterium) from the tops of their heads when provoked. The clearly visible osmeteria give off a pungent, repulsive odor which serves as a double warning to investigating predators.

As a caterpillar eats, it expands and soon outgrows its rigid outer covering, or exoskeleton. Beneath the exoskeleton a new "skin" forms of the same tough material called chitin. Before shedding its old skin, or molting, a caterpillar typically remains stationary on a plant for as long as a day without eating. Finally, when the exoskeleton reaches its limit of flexibility, the caterpillar crawls out and returns to eating. A caterpillar usually molts four or five times before entering its chrysalis stage, and butterfly gardening will give you many opportunities to watch this fascinating process.

The seemingly magical transformation from caterpillar to chrysalis

*Stages in the life cycle of the Anise Swallowtail: (clockwise from top) egg; early and late instar caterpillars; caterpillar ready to pupate; pupa; adult emerging from pupal case; courtship; mating; oviposition.*

22

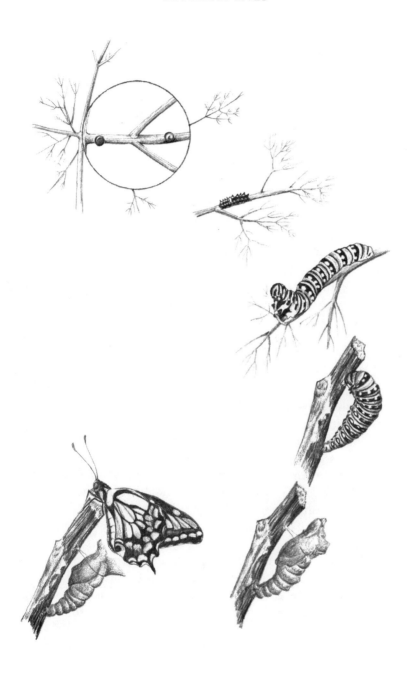

23

is sudden and complete. First a fully grown caterpillar stops feeding and searches—sometimes for the better part of a day—for a secluded or sheltered place to pupate, often the eave of an old barn, the stem of a nearby plant, or a hidden dead leaf of its food plant. Then it spins a tiny pad of silk on the substrate into which it hooks its anal prolegs. Finally, it molts for the last time, but this time, instead of a larger caterpillar emerging, a chrysalis appears.

## THE CHRYSALIS

The appearance of the chrysalis also varies from species to species, and keen observers can identify butterflies from their chrysalises just as they tell plants by their leaves or flowers. The chrysalis of the Mourning Cloak hangs upside down and has thorny spines along its light-brown body. The Variegated Fritillary also hangs upside down, but features black, orange, and yellow spots on a pearly blue-green background. The Falcate Orangetip looks like a long, green bud and hangs rightside up, supported by a silken girdle. Even the texture of pupal cases is distinctive. The Monarch's case, composed of a clear, smooth, wafer-like material, crackles like thin plastic when the butterfly emerges. The Gulf Fritillary's case, on the other hand, is like a fragile dead leaf and is virtually silent during eclosion.

During the pupal stage, phenomenal changes take place inside the chrysalis. First the caterpillar breaks down into a viscous substance. The cells of the butterfly are activated, sparking the development of the wings, head, thorax, and abdomen. You can see the beginnings of tiny but developed wings within some pupae after only four or five days. In a curious display of its living contents, a chrysalis will girate if you touch it and may ward off a wandering caterpillar or a potential predator by repeatedly thrusting itself ninety degrees to each side of its vertical, upside down position.

Shortly before a butterfly emerges, the appearance of its chrysalis changes noticeably. The clear wing cases of the Cabbage Butterfly turn from green to white, and the black patch on the corner of the forewing becomes visible. A day or so before the Gulf Fritillary hatches, its light-brown chrysalis begins to darken and take on a reddish hue that gradually deepens and envelops the entire chrysalis. Perhaps no butterfly exhibits a more dramatic change in chrysalis coloration than the regal Monarch, which turns from jade to pale green to dark orange to jet black within some nine hours.

## THE ADULT

Although most species hatch from their chrysalises in ten to fourteen days, some overwinter as pupae (a period known as diapause) and hatch the following season. Most emerge in the morning in order to take advantage of the day's sun. Immediately after hatching, a butterfly's body is immense and swollen, and its wings appear crumpled and deformed. A few minutes later, pumped up and flattened out by bodily fluids, the butterfly's wings assume their full size, and its body shrinks to its proper proportions. A newly hatched butterfly holds its wings slightly apart for an hour or more, allowing them to dry, before it makes its first flight into the world.

Since it cannot yet fly, the period just after emergence is the best time to observe the pristine condition of a butterfly unravaged by wind or the sharp edges of leaves and branches. Dr. Charles Hogue, Curator of Entomology at the Natural History Museum of Los Angeles County, likens the coloration of a butterfly's wings to the pointillist paintings of impressionist Georges Seurat. "In addition to the unbelievable brillance of many of their pure colors," he marvels, "different hues are contrastingly combined and blended in almost breathtaking designs. And the effects are always created, in the true pointillistic manner, by the allegiance of thousands of color points—the microscopic scales covering the otherwise transparent wing membrane on both upper and lower surfaces."

Two types of butterfly scales, pigmented and structural, overlap like roof shingles to produce the varied, kaleidoscopic coloration of a butterfly's wings. Pigmented scales appear brown, black, yellow, orange, white, or red in color. Structural scales appear blue, silver, purple, violet, or green in hue and refract light to produce a metallic or iridescent sheen. Viewed through a magnifying glass, the scales appear as exquisite, shining rectangles of yellow, blue, orange, silver, and many other hues.

The males of many species also have sex scales, or androconia, on their wings. Distinguishable as small black patches (stigmata) or as narrow strips, androconia disperse scent hormones, or pheromones, that are

25

produced by glands in the wings for mate communication. The black patches on the Monarch male's hindwings are good examples of androconia. A butterfly's scales can easily be rubbed off, leaving a powder on your fingers and the insect's wings transparent. While the loss of scales causes no harm in itself, a butterfly so handled may be fatally damaged.

## FLIGHT

In preparation for its first flight, a butterfly opens and closes its wings repeatedly to dry and warm them. Then, suddenly, its body quivers and the insect rises from its perch and flutters up into the air. Although to us the flight of a butterfly seems inspired only by whim, actually each species follows a unique and instinctive flight pattern. These patterns range from the darting dash of the skippers to the lilting ease of the Monarch. The Cabbage Butterfly bobs along frenetically, while the Gulf Fritillary sails gently by like the moon running through clouds. The Gray Hairstreak zips up and down like a pestering fly, and the Marine Blue flutters in tiny circles around a trellis of sweet peas. Swallowtails glide amiably across yawning spaces, while the Painted Lady travels hurriedly to its next appointment.

Butterflies usually take to the wing only when the sun is out. Scientists attribute this phenomenon to the sun's warming effect and speculate that orientation and decreased risk of storms may also be crucial. On sunny days, temperatures in the low- to mid-sixties will bring butterflies out. But on cloudy days, temperatures even into the low-seventies are inadequate. In fickle weather, the sudden disappearance of your yard's usually gregarious butterflies may indicate the arrival of clouds or an impending storm.

The poetic perception that butterflies simply waft away their lives in careless reverie is entirely false, for their entire repertoire of behavior follows defined, instinctive patterns.

## TERRITORIALITY

Territorial behavior is common among butterflies, as it is among vertebrates. I once repeatedly flushed a Fiery Skipper from its perch on an evergreen shrub. Each time, it returned within moments to the very same leaf from which it had been frightened away. Buckeyes and West

Coast Ladies also frequently return to the same patch of bare ground, and Mourning Cloaks settle again and again onto the same tree-branch perch.

Perching and patrolling are two typical butterfly stances. Those which perch, like the Pearly Crescentspot, take their positions on a single strategic branch or clod of earth and fly out to investigate inter-lopers. Scientists speculate that the Pearly Crescentspot's particularly pugnacious attacks may be motivated by its instinct to mate with what may be fleeting females, or alternatively, by the instinct to drive away competing males. Patrollers, on the other hand, fly up and down in regular patterns staking their claims on less tangible territory, in search of females.

Although individual butterflies can hardly do serious damage to each other, they do sometimes battle ferociously. In his book *Near Horizons*, Edwin Way Teale describes a Red Admiral which attacked him repeatedly in defense of a coveted patch of sand. "Indeed," Teale recalls, "this particular butterfly appeared to have little fear in its make-up. On its swerving, swooping circuits of the hillside, it was ever on the alert for interlopers. It flew at a Monarch or Yellow Swallowtail far larger than itself, as quickly as at a Grayling or a Painted Lady. . . . It attacked me as fearlessly as it did the smallest rival butterfly."

## PUDDLING

Butterflies are also fond of sipping water from the damp banks of puddles and streams or even, as I once observed in an encounter on a damp path with a Marine Blue, from the moist surfaces of pebbles and earth. Sometimes flocks of swallowtails, sulphurs, skippers, or blues gather in one spot, forming "mud-puddle clubs". Like all creatures, butterflies need moisture, but they also crave the salt carried in liquids. You may even be able to tempt an otherwise reluctant rider with the perspiration on your finger, forehead, or nose. And a puddle in your garden may prove an effective invitation to thirsty butterflies.

## ROOSTING

Late in the afternoon but before the sun sets, butterflies find a well camouflaged roosting spot for the night. Most butterflies roost singly in shrubs, trees, thick foliage, or grasses, but others, like the Zebra Longwing (or Zebra Butterfly), bed down communally with others of their kind. Hidden from their predators, butterflies are able to rest peacefully through the dangerous night hours. In fact, they are so well camouflaged that the gardener who wishes to observe a roosting butterfly will probably have to watch it find its resting spot. I once saw a Gulf Fritillary settle into the shadows of some dead branches of a drooping melaleuca and fold its wings. Several feet away, it was virtually invisible, and I'm certain I would have missed it had I not sighted its bedtime preparations in the making.

## CAMOUFLAGE AND DIVERSION

Predators and parasitoids (insect parasites that consume their hosts, thus killing them) that feed on butterflies are numerous and varied. Spiders capture caterpillars, pupae, and adults; ants prey on eggs; dragonflies snatch adults out of the sky; and birds attack caterpillars and devour adults, spitting out the wings. Many species of flies and wasps parasitize eggs, caterpillars, and pupae. Braconid wasps, for instance, lay their eggs in young caterpillars. Later the wasp larvae bore their way out of the caterpillar's body, on which they have been feeding, and spin tiny, straw-colored cocoons atop their victims. The mortally wounded caterpillar dies shortly thereafter. Chalcid wasps bore through the soft case of the newly formed chrysalis and lay their eggs inside. The wasp larvae feed on the chrysalis contents and later tunnel their way out, leaving behind a telltale hole in the lifeless pupal case.

To cope with these hazards, butterflies have evolved numerous camouflage and diversionary features which increase their survival rates. Clearly visible spots, markings, and tails serve as targets which divert gullible predators away from more vulnerable body parts. The Buckeye, for instance, has three large, bluish-purple eyespots along the edges of its wings, which might be mistaken for real eyes. Hairstreaks sport tails and have bright spots or false heads on the undersides of their hindwings. When at rest, they rub their hindwings back and forth, drawing attention to the spots. Swallowtails divert bird attacks away from their bodies to their more obvious, bright-spotted wingtails, which are frequently lost to the duped predator with no mortal damage done.

Particular masters of disguises are the rough-edged butterflies, in-

*Dangers are everywhere: a Cabbage White falls prey to a warbler, chalcid wasps emerge from an Anise Swallowtail chrysalis.*

cluding the Comma, Satyr Anglewing, and the closely related Mourning Cloak. The brown- or gray-mottled undersides of these butterflies' wings blend in so well with tree trunks that when the butterflies land, folding the wings together above their bodies, they become virtually invisible. Their jagged-edged wings further mask them as old tattered leaves. Some species even drop to the ground and play dead as if they were leaves! Moreover, their contrasting uppersides serve as a warning signal, which in sudden flight may startle a bird momentarily, giving the butterfly time to escape.

Coloration can also draw attention to a butterfly. Birds regurgitate after eating the unpalatable Monarch and after that rarely fail to heed the butterfly's orange and black warning. Like many species, the Viceroy has evolved coloration that mimics a similar toxic species. Almost a twin to the Monarch, the Viceroy feeds on non-toxic plants and is perfectly edible. But birds that have learned to avoid the Monarch also avoid the Viceroy.

## COURTSHIP

Orange and Common Sulphurs circling high over an alfalfa field are a common sight to farmers, but many people probably don't know that this familiar spectacle signals an early stage of butterfly courtship.

During courtship, the aggressive males buzz females, fly up into the air with them if they prove receptive, and then follow them down to a perch. Here, a courtship "dance" ensues. Robert Michael Pyle reports in *The Audubon Society Handbook for Butterfly Watchers*, that the distinctive steps of these minuets allow members of the same species to recognize each other and thus avoid crossbreeding. The male and female often circle each other and touch their antennae to each other's wings or abdomens. Females smell the males' pheromones with their antennae, either in the air or by brushing up against the males' androconia, and this makes them more receptive to mating. When the female is ready, the male positions himself behind her (back to back) and connects his

*Some butterfly defenses: the Comma's camaflouged wings, the Buckeye's deceptive eyespots, and the Giant Swallowtail's foul-smelling, hornlike osmeterium.*

30

abdomen to hers. Mating lasts from twenty minutes to two hours, and sometimes even overnight, and during that time the pair will sometimes continue to fly around and feed, remaining all the while connected. An already mated or unreceptive female tells interested males she is not available by rapidly fluttering or buzzing her wings or by raising her abdomen toward the sky.

## EGG LAYING

Female butterflies begin laying eggs within hours of mating and may continue over a number of days or even weeks. Prior to laying them, the female scouts out the food plant and the location on the plant which will best nourish her brood, a deliberate hovering and investigative activity which you might observe in your garden. Although sight and pattern recognition appear to play some role in identifying the proper host, Samuel Hubbard Scudder claims that smell is the sense primarily responsible for the correct host choice. Extrapolating from the significance of odors in mate attraction, Scudder speculates that the odors produced by the appropriate host plant may elicit the egg-laying response from a sensitized female.

Taste, a sense not often associated with insects, must also not be ignored. The tarsi located at the ends of the hindlegs are the taste organs of butterflies. By scratching the leaves of plants with their tarsi, females sense the chemicals contained in the plant and instinctively know whether those chemicals are suitable for its caterpillars.

As evidence of butterflies' sensitivity to taste, E. B. Ford, in his book *Butterflies*, reports that a butterfly almost always unrolls its proboscis when one of its hindlegs is immersed in an apple juice/water solution, but unrolls it only once in three times when the tarsus is not immersed in the liquid. Ford concludes that "while the butterfly is capable of perceiving the scent of the juice, it is much more stimulated if it can touch it." Alexander Klots, author of *1001 Answers to Questions About Insects*, confirms Ford's research, noting that Monarchs respond to sugar solutions of .0003 percent, indicating a taste sensitivity 1408 times greater than that of humans.

Having found the proper host plant, the female flutters above it, gently drops down, and while resting briefly on a leaf, stem, or flower head, swings her abdomen up and deposits a moist, glistening egg. The

Pearly Crescentspot, Baltimore, and Mourning Cloak lay their eggs in small groups or clusters of hundreds. The Comma and Question Mark lay theirs in vertical columns of three to ten eggs each. The Great Spangled Fritillary and some of its cousins lay their eggs near as well as on the food plant, while some browns haphazardly drop their eggs in the vicinity of the food plant. Most butterflies, however, lay their eggs singly and on the underside of the food plant leaf, where they will be protected from sun and predators.

## THE OBSERVANT GARDENER

Butterflies can be approached and watched from a very short distance in any of the attitudes described here. Remember that you are less likely to frighten them if you approach them from the side or below, since anything coming from above could be mistaken for a predator. Besides observing the behaviors which make up the complicated life cycle of Lepidoptera, you will, or course, want to engage in simple aesthetic observation and, perhaps, compile an imaginative account of your butterfly friends' personal idiosyncrasies. The prim grooming gestures of a Monarch may remind you of an eminently proper socialite. A Buckeye shaking its head from side to side and occasionally tilting its palpi out will look as though it's yawning and trying to wake itself up. And a butterfly sipping meditatively from blossom after blossom on a single flower head may reflect your own contemplative activity—taking in the contributing beauty of each of your butterfly visitors.

# REGIONS AND SEASONS

In Newfoundland, The Memorial University Botanical Garden at Oxen Pond provides larval food plants and nectar sources especially for local butterflies. Of the forty-eight butterfly species living on the island, twenty-six have been sighted in the garden. Curator Bernard Jackson reports that along with wide-ranging species like the Monarch, Cabbage Butterfly, and Painted Lady, the garden attracts regional or primarily northern species like the Short-tailed Swallowtail, Pink-edged Sulphur, Prairie Ringlet, Jutta Arctic, Northern Blue, and Arctic Skipper.

Thousands of miles west in Seattle, Washington, entomologist Sharon Collman selects common Pacific Northwest butterflies—Clodius Parnassian, Veined White, Ocher Ringlet, and Woodland Skipper—for her butterfly garden. And several latitudes to the south, Julian Donahue, Assistant Curator of Entomology at the Natural History Museum of Los Angeles County, recommends regional species like the West Coast Lady, Acmon Blue, and California Dogface to local butterfly gardeners.

These examples demonstrate the strict regionality of many butterfly species in contrast to the broad ranges of other species. The Monarch, Orange Sulphur (or Alfalfa Butterfly), and Cabbage Butterfly are found nearly everywhere in North America, but the Comma ranges almost exclusively in the East, the Sara Orangetip in the West, and the Queen in the South. The most common butterflies in your area may not be the most widespread species and may be quite rare or altogether absent a short distance away. Consequently, your own observations and research into local butterfly residents may provide the best guide in designing a successful butterfly garden.

Biogeographic life zones described primarily by latitude and altitude can be used as a model for butterfly distribution. The following table shows the location and representative inhabitants of North America's seven life zones.

| ZONE | LOCATION | AVERAGE MIDSUM- MER TEMP. | REPRESENTATIVE SPECIES |
|---|---|---|---|
| Tropical | Southernmost part of Florida, Texas, Arizona, and California | 80°F+ | Polydamas Swallowtail, Zebra Longwing, and Julia |
| Lower Austral | Deep South and southern Southwest | 78.8°F+ | Palamedes Swallowtail, Gulf Fritillary, and Pearly Eye |
| Upper Austral | Diagonal strip from New Jersey to northern Georgia, 40–43° latitude across central states, the Great Basin, parts of Southwest | 71.6– 78.8°F | Regal Fritillary, Diana, and Smoky Eyed Brown |
| Transition | Northern states and Appalachia | 64.4– 71.6°F | Baltimore, White Admiral, and Silverbordered Fritillary |
| Canadian | Horizontal strip across central Canada, and mountainous areas in Northeast, Appalachia, Rockies, and Sierra Nevada | 57.2– 64.4°F | Faunus Anglewing, Hoary Comma, and Atlantis Fritillary |
| Hudsonian | Across northern Canada and higher mountain altitudes in Northeast and Rockies | 50–57.2°F | Old World Swallowtail, Jutta Arctic, and Yukon Blue |
| Arctic-Alpine | Far North and above the treeline on mountains | 42.8–50°F | White Mountain Butterfly, Polaris Dingy Frittilary, and Behr's Sulphur |

Temperature, affected by altitude, latitude, and distance from the sea, largely determines how long during the year butterflies will remain on the wing. Those in the South, therefore, are generally visible for several seasons, while those in the North may appear for only a few weeks each year. Rainfall is also an important factor, because it heavily influences the types of plants which grow in a given area. The majority of butterflies prefer the moderate climes between wet and dry extremes.

Specific habitat preferences also govern the distribution of butterflies. Anglewings, for instance, harbor in forest edges, roads, and glades. Some fritillaries take best to grassy prairies, while others prefer mountain meadows. The Woodland Skipper and the Large Wood Nymph (despite their names) prefer the grassy areas which contain their food plants. Other butterflies thrive in areas that through man's interference or nurturing support ideal food plants for butterflies. These include abandoned railway lines, vacant lots, roadsides, alfalfa fields, and your garden.

Butterflies react to seasonal as well as regional factors and instinctively know when to hatch, mate, and emigrate to certain territories. Within each species, the number of generations born in a year is largely dependent on climate and genetic inheritance. Hence, species which range over more than one region may produce fewer broods in the nothern parts of their ranges than they do in the southern. In the North and Midwest, one or two generations is normal, but in the Sun Belt, most species have three or four broods. In the extreme South, four of five generations is not uncommon, while a single brood every one or two years prevails in the Arctic.

Generally, species which breed more often are more readily visible on the wing, but broods with particularly long-living individuals can also be observed for many months of the year. Members of the migratory fall generation of the Monarch, for instance, live six to eight months, and the hibernating Mourning Cloak and Comma may live more than nine months.

Early spring butterflies include the Checkered White, Sara and Falcate Orangetips, Silvery Blue, Satyr Anglewing, Buckeye, and Spring Azure. In late spring or summer look for the Giant Swallowtail, Dogface Butterfly, Great Spangled Fritillary, American Painted Lady, and White Admiral. In late summer or fall, the Pine White, Leonardus Skipper, and autumn generation of the Monarch may be seen in their respective regions.

35

*Regional butterflies (clockwise from top): White Admiral (N), Comma (E), Zebra Longwing (S), and West Coast Lady (W).*

## GETTING THROUGH THE WINTER

Butterflies hibernate in all four life stages depending on the species. Swallowtails will sometimes lie dormant for an entire year before hatching, while many Hairstreaks routinely overwinter as eggs. The young caterpillars of the Viceroy, White Admiral, and Red-spotted Purple construct hibernaculi in the fall by rolling up willow leaves into tubes, and securing them to the twigs with silk to prevent their falling off. In the spring, the caterpillars leave their shelters and begin to feed on the new growth of the willows. Most swallowtails, whites, and blues overwinter as chrysalises. Anglewings, Tortoiseshells, and the dusky Mourning Cloak hibernate through the cold season in hollow trees, crevices, or open barns, and are occasionally seen taking off-season joyrides on a mild January breeze by lucky passersby.

## EMIGRATION AND MIGRATION

Some species, including the Buckeye, American Painted Lady, and Red Admiral, extend their ranges northward during the summer months and die off in the fall, only to recolonize the region the following year. Favorable reproductive conditions may yield great swarms of these aerial emigrants, so that in certain years huge flocks of Painted Ladies fly north and east from Mexico and the Southwest. Overpopulation may be the primary motivation for the occasional flight of southern butterflies like the Gulf Fritillary, Dwarf Yellow, Cloudless Giant Sulphur, and Long-tailed Skipper, to northern climes. Most species tend either toward no-madism or domesticism. The Western Pygmy Blue wanders unpredictably around several western states, while the Zebra Swallowtail remains stubbornly in its original area.

Only the Monarch, however, possesses true bird-like migration. From September to October, great swarms of Monarchs make their way

*The Baltimore, which favors wet meadows, is shown here with turtlehead, its food plant, and purple loosestrife.*

*Mourning Cloaks overwinter as adults and often seek shelter in open structures such as sheds and barns.*

from New England, the Eastern Seaboard, and the Midwest to their winter destinations thousands of miles away in Mexico. These millions overwinter in fir forests high in the mountains. Tens of thousands of western slope Monarchs annually spend the winter clinging to eucalyptus trees in groves along the California coast.

Early in March, the Monarchs become active again, mate, and begin their journey east and north. Along the way, the females lay their eggs on milkweed plants, which nurture several fast summer generations. In the fall, the last of these summer generations repeats the great migration. But what force guides these new generations safely through their continental passage remains locked in the still unsolved mystery of instinct.

A butterfly garden along the route of the Monarch's migration may serve the butterflies with a valuable refueling station and breeding ground,

38

and may serve you with a fascinating observation post. But even if your garden doesn't lie in the Monarch's path, a variety of other species are bound to discover the vegetation and nectar you cultivate especially for them. So whether you're catering to the Miami Blue or the Colorado Anglewing, the California Dogface or the Ozark Swallowtail, you'll need to design your garden carefully to satisfy the butterflies' tastes, and that will be the subject of the next chapter.

*Butterfly gardens can be created in small spaces such as this patio. Potted plants make for quick and easy changes.*

FOUR

# GETTING STARTED

$I$n *Create a Butterfly Garden*, L. Hugh
Newman describes the sunny, south-facing, terraced hillside where he
allows wildflowers, grasses, and a large nettlebed to grow uncut until
autumn in order to provide a steady supply of nectar sources and larval
food plants for the butterflies which visit his British garden. Cultivated
flowers complement the wild plants, and hedges and bushes furnish shelter. The garden is both sun splashed and shade dappled, and its owner
avoids using insecticides entirely. "I have, over a number of years,"
Newman explains, "deliberately tried to produce conditions that butterflies like."

The Drum Manor Butterfly Garden in Northern Ireland was built
in the walled garden of an old Irish estate turned public park. The nearly
twelve-foot wall, erected to protect the vegetable beds from the harsh
maritime winds, now shelters butterflies. Tall trees provide further protection. "There are many hazy days in summer when it takes the shelter
of a south-facing wall or wood border to tempt most butterflies into
activity," reports former Queen's University of Belfast Professor Henry
George Heal.

These two successful butterfly gardens illustrate how important it is
to provide the environment butterflies in your region need for survival,
including not only nectar sources and larval food plants, but adequate
sunlight, shelter, and water, which are just as essential. The closer your
garden matches the natural habitat, the greater your chances of attracting
and convincing butterflies to stay. Nevertheless, creativity and imagination should always be the guideposts for your gardening. The possible

*41*

# GETTING STARTED

*Butterfly garden features: sunlight, shelter, puddles, a rocky area, a meadow, and of course nectar and food sources.*

combinations of butterfly species, wildflowers, domestic plants, exotic vegetation, annuals, perennials, trees, vines, vegetables, and garden designs are endless, and one or more of them are sure to be right for both you and your location.

## FIRST STEPS

But where to begin? Your first goal is to select which butterfly species you would like to attract and which plants are likely to draw them. Survey your neighborhood for resident species, and make note of what plants they are most often seen on. Experts at your local natural history museum or college may also offer some good advice. If you are fortunate enough to have a local entomology club, members who have been observing butterflies in your area for years will probably be delighted to share their knowledge.

Your garden's latitude, altitude, exposure to sun and wind, rainfall, atmospheric and soil conditions, and proximity to urban or rural areas will determine its complexion. But these are constraints all gardeners must cope with and can be advantages as well as disadvantages. By learning the specific habitats of particular species and whether those habitats can be incorporated into your yard, you will know which butterflies might establish themselves in your garden. Passion flower (or passion vine) in southern cities is attractive to the Gulf Fritillary, and vacant lots tangled with cheeseweed are often frequented by the West Coast Lady. But the Diana and the Olympia Marblewing will scarcely be found in such urban settings, preferring Appalachian forests and the shale barrens of rocky river bluffs respectively.

## DESIGNING YOUR GARDEN: SUN

Large, open spaces filled with sunlight are an important element of any butterfly garden, since butterflies are most active in sunny areas. The center of the garden is often the most convenient area for sunshine, but corners may be used as well. Ground cover such as clover, alfalfa, or other low-growing host or nectar plants combine well with grasses in open areas. Remember to leave room for nectar sources and food plants which should be planted around the open areas and still well in the sun. Different species of butterflies nectar at different times of the day, so you

*Wildflowers that serve as nectar sources include (clockwise from top left) goldenrod, cinquefoil, aster, dandelion, and bee balm.*

will want some nectar plants to be in the sun whenever they call. Rock gardens planted with sedum, aubrieta, and primrose do especially well in sunny locations and serve as ideal basking spots for warmth-loving butterflies.

## SHELTER

Walls or borders of shrubs or trees will provide adequate shelter from the wind for butterflies. It is not necessary to completely surround the garden with windbreaks, but ample protection will attract more butterflies. Shrubby nectar sources like butterfly bush, honeysuckle, and New Jersey tea, and food plants like spicebush, hawthorn, and hibiscus work nicely as windbreaks. Willow, poplar, and wild cherry trees offer additional shelter. On fences or trellises, hops, pipevine, and passion flower create wonderful windscreens and larval hosts. Painting a fence or board to match the colors of the butterflies which frequent the flowers in front of it may create a safe haven for camouflaged insects, as well as providing shelter. Certainly a patch of winter cress backed by a checkered fence and dotted with Checkered Whites will win the neighborhood prize for originality!

## PUDDLES

At least one and preferably several puddles should be provided for your butterfly guests. Gouging level surfaces or grading to create an incline will allow natural rains to rejuvenate these moisture sources. Wet

*Cultivated flowers that serve as nectar sources include (clockwise from left) daisy, lobelia, phlox, and ageratum.*

sand, earth, or mud are the best butterfly fountains, as butterflies cannot drink from open water. Susan Borkin, Assistant Curator of Invertebrate Zoology at the Milwaukee Public Museum in Wisconsin, suggests burying a bucket in the ground and filling it with sand to an inch or so from the top. Place a few rocks or sticks on top of the sand and fill the bucket with water. Butterflies will perch on the rocks or sticks and drink from the moist sand. Such an "instant puddle" is best situated in an open sunny area or along a path. Butterflies are also atracted to urine patches, so a spot that a pet visits makes an ideal puddling spot.

In her book *Theme Gardens*, Barbara Damrosch suggests grading the entire garden to create a bowl-like effect with a "tiny seasonal pond" in the center. Large flat stones placed in the pond will serve as perching and sun basking sites for butterflies and may attract them even on hazy days. And splashing the rocks with stale beer or a sugar- or honey-water solution will make them especially inviting.

## MEADOWS

The meadow habitat is popular with most butterflies and should be prominent in your garden. A sunny hillside meadow like L. Hugh Newman's will provide hiding places and host plants for eggs and larvae, wildflowers for nectaring adults, and a brimming pool of color for your aesthetic pleasure. Jo Brewer, a Massachusetts butterfly gardener, rototilled half her front lawn and planted meadow grasses, wildflower transplants, and assorted seeds. Soon her daisies, wild asters, yarrow, and thistles were bustling with butterflies.

The co-author of *The Butterfly Gardener*, Dr. Miriam Rothschild, has an acre of meadow in her English country garden. The fervent field scabious, knapweeds, and thistles furnish sufficient nectar to support breeding colonies of grass feeders like the Meadow Brown, Wall, Gatekeeper, and Small Skipper. "On warm evenings," gushes the doting gardener, "I walk through it [the hayfield] after dark and imagine it stretches away for thirty acres or more on all sides."

## TERRACES, BORDERS, BEDS, AND PATHWAYS

Placing tall plants in the rear of the garden with shrubs and flower beds in front, produces a terraced effect that provides shelter for your

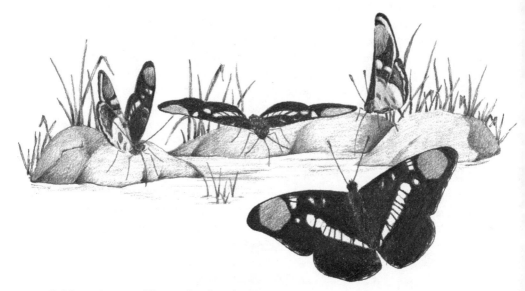

*California Sisters puddling at the edge of a stream.*

butterflies and allows you an unimpeded view of all the garden's activity. Similarly, a graded hillside covered with flower beds enhances "the feeling of being inside a bowl of color, some of it fixed and some of it hovering in flight," says Barbara Damrosch.

Perennials and annuals planted in front of a stone wall or wooden fence provide nectaring and basking sites, and soften the stark edges of such artificial structures. Marigolds, zinnias, and impatiens are examples of long-blooming annuals that can be used individually or together to create beautiful borders that require little care. A number of small flower beds scattered throughout a garden may be more suitable for urban or suburban gardens and will serve as tasty oases for butterflies without dominating the landscape.

Art Douglas, a California butterfly gardener, uses baby's tears, a food plant of the Red Admiral, as ground cover in flower beds. Sweet alyssum and ageratum also provide excellent ground cover and serve as tempting nectar sources for many species. Pathways, driveways, and alleys beneath groves of trees serve as butterfly highways, and bordered with nectar sources and larval food plants will encourage butterflies to dawdle rather than cruise.

## WINDOW BOXES AND PLANTERS

Window boxes or potted plants hung along a fence place nectar sources in a position that is easier for butterflies to see and reach. Stephen Austin's butterfly garden in El Monte, California, features a purple *Lantana montevidensis* that nearly covers a six-foot-high fence. When I visited, skippers, Cabbage Butterflies, and Gulf Fritillaries flocked to the elevated nectar source. An urban dweller's window box, planted with primroses, zinnias, verbena, and alyssum will attract a variety of equally colorful butterflies, across the paved streets to the oasis of his apartment windowsill. You will probably be surprised at the number of butterflies that somehow survive in an urban environment, and a well positioned window box will serve as haven in the city for them.

## SOILS

Wildflowers, a main component of butterfly gardens, grow best in soils which approximate their natural habitats. Forest and wetland plants generally prefer acidic soils, while many desert flowers grow best in alkaline soil. Fortunately, the meadow and prairie flowers that butterflies like best usually flourish in neutral soils similar to normal garden soil. But unlike cultivated plants, many wildflowers grow in porous, sandy soil. Mulching or adding sand to your soil may be a necessary conditioning step. A soil test will determine the chemical makeup of your soil and indicate whether you need to add leaf mold or sulphur to make it more acidic, or lime to make it more alkaline.

In their book *Wildflower Gardening*, James Underwood Crockett and Oliver Allen suggest burying nine-inch-wide rigid, plastic or rust-resistant metal bands flush with the soil surface around flower beds in order to keep undesired chemicals from invading the soil. A band two inches away from a lime-containing masonry wall and separated from the wall by a sand buffer will keep alkaline chemicals away from the rest of the garden. This technique is especially valuable for butterfly gardens, which frequently have walls. Also pay attention to variations in soil conditions within your garden and plant wildflowers, shade plants, and marsh grasses accordingly.

*49*

## DISCOURAGING BIRDS AND PESTS

Hugh Newman cautions butterfly gardeners not to provide nesting boxes for birds which prey on butterflies and damage flowers and fruit. Swallows, housemartins, flycatchers, and sparrows are particularly fond of butterflies, and tits are known to eat caterpillars. Avoid cultivating plants which have fruits or seeds that birds eat and which do not attract butterflies, as birds may prey on your garden's guests. Keep in mind too that hackberry, blueberry, spicebush, hawthorn, dogwood, juniper, alfalfa, clover, asters, honeysuckle, viburnum, sumac, sunflowers, daisies, marigold, zinnia, and butterfly weed attract both butterflies and birds. Protective covering in the form of a thin loosely draped netting will reduce the number of eggs, caterpillars, and pupae that fall prey to birds.

Instead of using insecticides and herbicides, use selective pest-control methods and encourage the propagation of ladybird beetles and other insects that prey on garden pests. Adrian Wenner of Santa Barbara, California uses a menagerie of traps, gadgets, and devices to keep pests out of his garden. In the space of ten weeks he caught more than 1600 walnut husk flies in a number of traps hung in fruit and nut trees. Punctured film canisters containing ammonium carbonate chunks also attract and kill flies. Sticky tape around the trunks of his dwarf naval orange trees keeps ants from going up the trunks and protecting scale insects and aphids from predators and parasitoids. This allows ladybird beetles to fly in and prey on the scale insects and aphids. Meanwhile Monarchs and Gulf Fritillaries soar unimpeded around his milkweeds and passion flower.

## LIVESTOCKING

Stocking is an effective way to encourage large butterfly garden populations. Eggs, caterpillars, or, with more difficulty, pupae can be obtained from the wild, and a few species in various stages can be bought from butterfly suppliers. Eggs or caterpillars found in the wild can be brought back to your garden and placed on appropriate food plants. Eggs or pupae should not be removed from the leaf they are found on. Instead, the entire leaf or branch should be removed and transported to the new location. Alternatively, catch a mature female (most will already have mated) and place it in a cage along with some potted or cut food plant, cut flower heads, and a shallow dish full of tissue paper saturated with sugar water. Within a few days she will lay her eggs and can then be released.

## CAUTION ON EXOTIC BUTTERFLIES

Exotic species of butterflies should not be introduced to gardens outside of their natural regions. In the absence of natural enemies, they are likely to become pests and may damage the gene pools of native fauna or disrupt the biogeographical records of scientists. Since its introduction to Quebec from Europe in 1860, the Cabbage Butterfly has created a nuisance for farmers and gardeners who raise crucifers. Newly introduced butterflies that flourish in the absence of natural enemies may decimate indigenous plant species and compete mercilessly with native butterfly species. Moreover, any diseases, parasites, or parasitoids they carry could harm endemic flora and fauna. The U.S. Department of Agriculture strictly regulates the importation and interstate transportation of "noxious weeds" and plant pests (including butterflies), as do state and local agencies. These regulations should be unerringly respected.

## SPECIAL TOUCHES

Unique mini-environments may draw additional and, sometimes, less common species to your garden. A small wooded area will entice satyrs and Mourning Cloaks in from the wilds, and you can observe them from a convenient stump or well-placed bench. Buckeyes and Red-spotted Purples, which are fond of open trails, may be attracted to a patch of bare ground in a sun-dappled glade. One particularly enterprising gardener I visited was building a large mound of dirt in the center of his garden to simulate the mountainous habitat of some regional species. By placing large rocks on the mound and making other nooks and crannies, he hoped to attract butterflies in need of shelter from wind, heat, and cold. The watchword, as this butterfly gardener obviously knew, is imagination. Experimentation and creativity will yield an infinite number of garden designs, and one of them is bound to surprise you with the number of butterflies it engenders. But now that you've planned your garden design, you'll need to know just which nectar and larval food plants will best satisfy the butterflies' tastes and your own aesthetic criteria.

*51*

# NECTAR SOURCES

In 1950 a team of biologists from the New York Zoological Society began studying butterflies at a jungle field station in Trinidad. Seven years later, with the project continuing to yield valuable information about insect evolution, courtship, and habits, scientist Jocelyn Crane reported that butterflies

> are as particular about their food as a spoiled child getting over the measles. The morphos, for instance, would much rather eat rotten bananas than sip the sweetest nectar. The heliconiids prefer a diet of nectar from lantana plants. . . . Little by little we discovered the preferred foods of our more finicky guests. They don't like much variety; each kind goes to its own favorites, day after day, like a small girl who always orders chocolate sodas while her best friend sticks to vanilla malts.

Studies like the Trinidad project indicate that butterfly preferences are determined by a combination of the color, shape, and fragrance of flowers or other food sources. Many ornamental blossoms, and hybrids like roses and hydrangea, which often have no nectaries, are shunned by butterflies. But a variety of nectar sources appeal to many butterflies and, given prominence in your garden, may be the butterfly attraction of the neighborhood.

## COLOR SENSITIVITY

Color is an important determinant of preference, because butterflies have "the broadest [range of sensitivity to light wavelength] known of any animal," according to Dr. Gary Bernard, a Yale University scientist.

Unlike man, butterflies are able to see ultraviolet light. This sensitivity allows them to identify otherwise unremarkable flowers from a distance and to distinguish between blossoms which appear similar to the human eye. In a study conducted at Cornell University by Dr. Thomas Eisner and others, the dark centers of the marsh marigold which appeared only in ultraviolet photographs, taken by the researchers, were determined to act as "nectar guides" for butterflies which prefer the flower. Many flowers also have nectar guides that are visible to the human eye, in the form of lines or patterns that lead into the center of the flower where the nectaries are situated—the dark pink blotch in the center of some phloxes, for example. Species of flowers with nectar guides are more frequently visited than those without and, as a result, are more abundantly pollinated. Thus, the coevolution of butterflies which seek nectar guides and flowers which possess them benefits both forms of life.

Other photographs in the Eisner study showed that a group of five composites, which look similar to humans, have differently sized dark patches in the ultraviolet, making them distinguishable to butterflies. Eisner also indicates that butterfly markings that appear only in the ultraviolet highlight sexual dimorphism, facilitating communication between the genders in mating.

Spectral sensitivity also varies between species of butterflies, says Bernard. His studies show that several species, including the Question Mark, Sleepy Orange, Cloudless Giant Sulphur, and Eastern Tailed Blue, are sensitive to the longest red wavelengths, a trait which may make them prefer red flowers over others. The Hackberry Butterfly, Mourning Cloak, and Buckeye, among others, are not able to see these wavelengths.

Studies conducted by researchers C.A. and S.L. Swihart indicate that successful nectaring on a particular flower may also condition a butterfly's preference for that flower's color. In a series of experiments, the Swiharts fed butterflies on yellow model flowers that contained sponges soaked in a honey solution. Two days later, they replaced the yellow flowers with models in a variety of colors, and found that the conditioned butterflies visited yellow test models much more frequently than did unconditioned butterflies.

The shape of a particular flower may also make it more attractive to certain butterflies, either because it provides a convenient platform for perching or because the flower tubes are easily accessible to the

*A West Coast Lady uses a daisy's convenient landing platform while nectaring.*

butterfly. Most butterfly nectar sources have tubular flowers arranged around a flower head—for example, daisies—or in a cluster that provides ample space for landing and perching. Butterflies seldom use flowers that hang down from a vine or a stem, or double ornamental blossoms.

Although butterflies are willing experimenters, alighting on a variety of flowers before they give themselves over to particular species, there is a method to the madness of their final decisions. And those decisions usually reveal the most suitable match of butterfly and plant morphology. For example, as Paul Opler writes in his *Butterflies East of the Great Plains*, butterflies with short proboscises generally prefer short-tubed flowers, and butterflies with long proboscises use long-tubed flowers. As a rule, says Opler, butterflies visit flower tubes that are half as long as their proboscises. The length of the tubes of some flowers, like *Lantana camara*, may exclude butterflies with small proboscises from nectaring, because these butterflies can't reach into the nectaries. In a comparison of the different species of butterflies which feed on *Lantana camara* and *Lantana trifolia*, University of Illinois researcher Douglas Schemske theorized that the two plants evolved their differing tube sizes in order to separate their pollinators and ensure their own sympatric survival.

The relation of butterfly size to the size and availability of a perching platform on flowers also influences butterfly preferences. The large-winged swallowtails, for instance, opt for the wide, high platform of a daylily over low-lying alyssum. And though large flowers generally contain more nectar, small flowers situated in clusters on a stem have the advantage of allowing butterflies to extend their proboscises to many flowers without moving off the cluster. Large flowers, preferred by large butterflies, are usually found higher on the stem than smaller flowers, giving the butterflies ample room for fluttering their wings. Because most butterflies refuse to climb down into flowers where their wings may be damaged, butterflies with short proboscises usually shun deep, wide blossoms. Occasionally, however, certain blues or other butterflies will burrow down into a blossom to reach its recessed nectaries.

Fragrance is another component in nectar preference. Many of the most fragrant flowers—heliotrope, mignonette, lilac, lavender, sweet alyssum, viburnum—draw throngs of butterflies. And, as a rule, flowers with the same color and shape will be selected by butterflies in order of the strength of their fragrances.

To satisfy the greatest number of butterfly preferences, you'll probably find that the best menu to offer your butterfly customers is a well-

*This lantana's cluster of tubular flowers allows a Common Blue to obtain a large amount of nectar in a single visit.*

stocked soda fountain including flowers of all shapes, sizes, colors, and fragrances. And by mixing wildflowers, cultivated flowers, shrubs, and trees and planting them in a variety of locations and environments, you'll be able to tempt even the most finicky butterflies in your botanical café.

## RECOMMENDED NECTAR SOURCES

Successful butterfly gardeners integrate wild and cultivated flowers and use a combination of vegetation with staggered blooming seasons. Buddleia (or butterfly bush), orange milkweed (or butterfly weed), and lantana are by consensus the most popular butterfly attractants.

Cultivated plants such as daisies, asters, lobelia, sweet alyssum, verbena, phlox, scabiosa, and coreopsis are also strong choices. Wildflower varieties including goldenrod, Joe-Pye-weed, boneset, wild bergamot, and dandelion are prime nectar sources, and wild varieties of such cultivated plants such as phlox, verbena, and aster are other possibilities. There are some plants that serve dually as nectar sources and larval food plants; most common among them are clover, buckwheat, and thistle. Larger nectar sources that are especially effective for shelter or bordering include hawthorn, sumac, lilac, buckeye, and New Jersey tea. If you're interested in seasonal staggering, spring-blooming flowers include arabis, primrose, and lilac. Butterfly weed and yarrow come to flower during the hot months of summer, and in the late summer or early fall, butterfly bush, goldenrod, and sedum burst into blossom. Particularly long-blooming varieties include candytuft (spring through summer), phlox (summer into fall), and the everpresent dandelion. The blooming season of individual plants can be prolonged by periodic removal of dead blossoms, promoting the growth of new ones.

## SUCCESS WITH WILDFLOWERS

Wildflowers usually grow best if started from seed, which can be collected from nearby fields. Which types of wildflowers you select will depend on the soil conditions and climate of your region. Indigenous species are most likely to flourish, but before planting, consult local authorities about weed regulations that may prohibit certain varieties. Some species may establish themselves from wind-carried seed without your interference. Others will resist even the most painstaking care and

*Many types of plants serve as nectar sources. Clockwise from top left: Joe-Pye-weed, zinnia, hawthorn, coreopsis, clover, and candytuft.*

attention. Although wildflowers can be planted together with cultivated plants, many gardeners prefer to reserve an obscure corner of the garden for native species or to plant them in rows separate from lawns and cultivated plant beds. In addition to attracting throngs of butterflies, wildflowers once established require little ongoing care and add a natural flavor to your garden setting.

## ANNUALS AND PERENNIALS

Planting combinations of annuals and perennials gives the butterfly gardener the freedom to change a garden's appearance from year to year and assures him that some beds will sprout without replanting. Sweet alyssum, viper's bugloss, and mignonette are recommended annuals; sweet rocket, fleabane, and thrift are possible perennials. Remember too that both annuals and perennials occasionally spread to other parts of the garden and that perennials may not flower until the year after planting. Nectar sources that can be purchased as either annuals or perennials include candytuft, coreopsis, impatiens, lobelia, lupine, phlox, dianthus, sage, scabiosa, statice, sunflower, and toadflax.

Art Douglas's butterfly garden in Los Angeles displays an exemplary cornucopia of purple, lavender, blue, red, pink, orange, yellow, and white annuals and perennials. Oleander, impatiens, and lantana complement his marigolds, cosmos, ageratum, dianthus, and dwarf zinnias. A row of potted pansies smile amiably across the expanse of color. On my visit there, I observed a number of Fiery Skippers sipping from the marigolds and a striking Funereal Duskywing foraging on cosmos. A Cabbage Butterfly laid its eggs on the nasturtium, the flowers of which also provide nectar.

## GARDEN COLOR SCHEMES

As a gardener and butterfly enthusiast, you are an artist whose palette and subject matter are unequaled in variety and richness. And designing the color scheme of your garden gives you the opportunity to test the bounds of your creativity and indulge your most eccentric tastes. Vast expanses of snowy, violet, or rose-red blossoms can be painted with alyssum, candytuft, or sedum. Gold-and-crimson-streaked gaillardias or yellow marigolds and orange marigolds make an attractive confetti border. The cottony ocean-blue flowers of ageratum wave peacefully, like the waters of a sheltered inlet, on a quiet day. Pink and yellow Michaelmas daisies, or yellow and white Shasta daisies are an attractive and adaptable filler for yawning spaces. Lantana, which comes in several colors, can be matched to the color of your house, fence, or even the butterflies you hope it will attract. A Great Southern White adds a zesty splash to a bright, orange lantana. And imagine the delightful contrast of a Monarch's orange and black mantle on a tuft of goldenrod or a swatch of yellow daisies.

Gardens designed around a single color are another tantalizing option. Vita Sackville-West's famous all-white garden at Sissinghurst Castle in Kent, England features candytuft, lilies, dianthus, pansies, and irises among other butterfly nectar sources. Anthemis, marigold, sunflower, goldenrod, black-eyed Susan, beggar-ticks, buttercup, dandelion, common groundsel, ragwort, and toadflax could as easily be substituted for a yellow garden that would bring its own sunshine to cloudy days.

Remember too that nectar sources should be clumped together, as a greater density of flower heads is especially attractive to butterflies.

*Nectar sources have varying blooming seasons. Clockwise from bottom: arabis (spring), yarrow (summer), and marigold (late summer).*

Shrubs with a number of flowers or large beds are most visible to butterflies at a distance and, therefore, may draw more visitors from around the neighborhood.

## LEARNING FROM YOUR NECTAR SOURCES

Perhaps the best way to discover which nectar sources are preferred by the butterflies in your area is observation. Recorded favorites may not be the preference of the butterflies in your garden, and your own combinations may prove extremely popular with butterflies. Flowers which produce nectar late in the day instead of early may be especially attractive to late-flying butterflies. Butterflies may even prefer different colors of blossoms at different times of the year. A.H. Hamm spent five years recording the number of butterflies which visited a two-hundred-yard border of closely interspersed reddish-purple, purple, and white Michaelmas daisies on the grounds of the Cowley Road Hospital in Oxford, England. His tabulations indicate that, curiously, the butterflies preferred the reddish-purple blossoms until they passed the stage of full-bloom in the mid-October. Then, the butterflies chose the various shades of purple flowers. The white forms, Hamm observed, were consistently neglected.

## BEYOND FLOWERS

Many butterflies, including the White Admiral, Red-spotted Purple, Question Mark, Mourning Cloak, Red Admiral, Comma, and Viceroy, eschew flowers in favor of rotting fruit, tree sap, dung, carrion, urine, and other non-nectar sources of nutrients. If these species are particular favorites of yours, allow the fruit from your fruit trees to decay on the ground, leave your pet's droppings where they lie, or place a bit of raw lamb chop or fish in a discreet part of the garden.

Sugaring, a technique described in Robert Michael Pyle's *Handbook*, is a cleaner and somewhat less noxious way to tempt these elusive species. According to Pyle, a concoction of "a couple of pounds of sugar, a bottle or two of stale beer, mashed overripe bananas, some molasses or syrup, fruit juice, and a shot of rum," painted on trees, rocks, stumps or fence posts will draw an abundance of butterflies. To avoid the unattractive mess this mixture makes on trees and the mass of unwanted insects that it is likely to entrap, he suggests hanging mixture-soaked sponges from

*Some supplements to nectar sources: test-tube "flowers" and rotting fruit.*

convenient tree limbs. A large sponge or one suspended on a tray provides a good landing area for butterflies.

In the absence of fresh flowers, hungry butterflies can be treated to a soup of sugar-or honey-water. Hugh Newman recommends securing test tubes filled with the solution and plugged with cotton or paper toweling to stakes, a fence, or even the stem of a plant. A flower made of colored paper, opaque plastic, or other waterproof material and arranged around the mouth of the tube will provide a perching platform and a familiar color attractant for butterflies. With luck, the butterflies will mistake a bunch of these tubes and "petals" for a bush covered with delicious flowers.

These test tubes can also be set into holes in the top of a butterfly table, as described by Clive Farrell, director of the London Butterfly House. Farrell recommends a ten percent solution of white sugar in water, a five to ten percent solution of fructose in water, a maple syrup-water solution to imitate tree sap, or—for butterflies that crave salts—a salt-water solution. Take care not to make the solutions too strong as this might clog the butterflies' proboscises, and remember to clean the tubes at least every forty-eight hours.

Rotting fruits, like banana, pear, peach, pineapple, plum, apple, and orange, placed in one or more dishes on the table serve as additional attractants. Farrell notes that butterfly catchers in Malaysia and other butterfly-rich countries use "horse or cow manure, rotting prawns, or a dead rat or two," to bait their prey, but in the interests of your neighborhood and your nose, you may not want to use these items. A few dishes of sweetened solution scattered discreetly around the garden completes the smorgasbord of delectables for butterflies. Such supplementary sources of nourishment may prove particularly effective in early spring, late fall, or following periods of bad weather when blossoms are less available.

## BUTTERFLIES, BUTTERFLIES, BUTTERFLIES

When selecting nectar sources and artificial nutrients, the measure of success is, obviously, the number of butterflies you are able to gather. Australian Ethel Anderson, in a 1940 article in *The Atlantic Monthly*, boasted of the "fluttering thousands" of butterflies which outnumbered even the flowers in her garden. "I can see five Satyridae to each single dandelion. And on these lawns dandelions flourish like buttercups in Berkshire," she marveled.

Penciled Blues and Fiery Jewels dance above the china asters, and over the cactus dahlias, Clover Blues and Painted Ladies weave flight patterns prodigal in beauty. . . . On a Michaelmas daisy's lacy white and gold and green, three to a flower, wings up like sails, banked thick as Silver-washed Fritillaries in an English lane, succeeding fleets of Checkered Swallowtails ride at anchor, but are never still.

"If I were very rich," she concludes,

I would not have in my garden so very many trees (though I would have a good many), or flowers (though I would have some, planted like vegetables in a kitchen garden)—no; I would keep a scientist to procure me flights of butterflies.

"Every morning I should like my butler to say, 'The scientist, ma'am, is on the back doorstep, awaiting today's orders.' Then I would answer, 'Tell him, please, to release the perennial phlox fifty Tailed Cupids. Over the Prunus he could set free some Jezebels and Wood Whites, and take a covey of Lacewings and Leopards across to those hawthorns.' "

Even without Anderson's imaginary handy scientist, it's possible to have flocks of fluttering butterflies elbowing up to the well-stocked bar in your garden. And, after drinks comes the main course—the caterpillars' food plants. And that is what we will discuss next.

*There are many type of food plants. Clockwise from left: wildflowers (lupine), cultivated flowers (hibiscus), and grasses (Bermuda grass).*

# LARVAL FOOD PLANTS

"**I**'m not a green thumb, but I'm rather excited about growing a butterfly garden this spring in our back-yard," wrote *Los Angeles Times* columnist Jack Smith after learning that passion flower vine serves as the food plant for the Gulf Fritillary.

I thought back to springs past, when I had fought savagely but in vain against the passion vine that was violating our lovely pepper tree, seducing it with purple flowers and squeezing it lifeless in irresistible arms. . . . And all the time . . . the passion vine was surrendering its own flesh to my caterpillars, and in time it would be transformed into the lovely orange, black and silver fritillary that gave such color and motion to our acre. . . . I went down to look at the pepper tree, on our second level just at the edge of the canyon, to see if the vine was back. I hoped so. I hated to think of a summer without butterflies.

Many gardeners, like Smith, have no idea that certain plants in their yards—milkweed, thistle, nettle, clover—which they have worked so diligently to get rid of support butterfly larva or that destroying the plants will also decimate the garden's butterfly population. But a close inspection of such plants will reveal a variety of larval species, which, like the garden's flowers, will soon burst into the bloom of maturity.

## GENERALISTS AND SPECIALISTS

Just as adult butterflies display preferences in nectar sources, caterpillars feed on a limited number of food plants, the constituents of which are required for healthy development. The number of adequate food plants varies from species to species. Some species frequent a variety of food plants, while others feed only on closely related members of the same plant family, and still others require a specific genus or even species of plant.

Species that eat a variety of food plants, like the Gray Hairstreak, Buckeye, Painted Lady, Comma, and Mourning Cloak, usually select the plants which at a given time of the year or in a specific region or habitat are most succulent and abundant. Consequently, each generation of the Spring Azure, which feeds on food plants with staggered flowering seasons, uses a different combination of food plants. In Northern Virginia, reports Paul Opler, the first generation chooses common dogwood and wild cherry, while the second generation chooses New Jersey tea, osier dogwood, and viburnum. Similarly, the northern Baltimore feeds on turtlehead, while the southern variety chooses beardtongue. Larry Orsak found that "the Bright Blue Copper is found on the canyon floors but never on the south slopes," because the butterfly's food plant, common buckwheat, receives more water on the canyon floor and therefore puts out more growth and larger leaves than its siblings on the adjacent arid slopes. Orsak also discovered that the same butterfly species uses only three of sixty-five possible buckwheat species in southern California, because the females prefer the large succulent leaves of the favored trio.

Related butterflies often feed on closely related members of the same plant families. Some of these are the Monarch and Queen which feed on milkweeds; most whites which feed on mustards; fritillaries which feed on violets; sulphurs which feed on clovers; the Comma, Question Mark, and Satyr Anglewing which feed on nettles; the Eastern Black and Anise Swallowtails which feed on members of the carrot family; and the Viceroy, White Admiral, and Red-spotted Purple which feed on willows.

Most common butterflies which thrive discriminately on a single food plant feed on one with a wide range, as their population growth would otherwise be severely impeded. These specialists include some small blues which use a single species of buckwheat for both food plant and nectar source.

*Thistle and other "weeds" are popular food plants and nectar sources for the Painted Lady and other butterflies.*

## PLANNING FOOD PLANTS

Before planting food plants, consult other local butterfly gardeners, regional field guides, your area's natural history museum or entomologists, and the appendix of this book to find out which food plants are frequented by butterflies in your area. Remember, again, that butterfly-food plant matches vary from region to region, so the "official" preference may not apply in your garden. Although Painted Ladies usually feed on thistles, they may flourish in your succulent mallow patch. And while the Viceroy is generally fond of willows, it may find your poplar and aspen just as inviting.

## CULTIVATED PLANTS

Although wild plants compromise the majority of caterpillar food plants, several cultivated varieties also serve as butterfly hosts. Some which you might try are nasturtium, host to the Cabbage Butterfly;

hibiscus, frequented by the Gray Hairstreak; violets, which fritillaries enjoy; spicebush, host to the Spicebush Swallowtail; hawthorn, eaten by both the White Admiral and the Red-spotted Purple; cassia, food of the Cloudless Sulphur and the Sleepy Orange; hollyhock, frequented by the Painted Lady; and passion flower, which, as you now know, is the food of the Gulf Fritillary. Trees—elm for the Mourning Cloak and Question Mark, sycamore for the Western Tiger Swallowtail, pawpaw for the Zebra Swallowtail, citrus for the Giant Swallowtail—are also caterpillar havens. And several lawn grasses, like Bermuda grass and St. Augustine grass, sustain satyrs and skippers.

Ty Garrison's Los Angeles garden features a single cultivated food plant—a gigantic passion flower vine that curls along a fence and rises fifteen to twenty feet off the ground, covering a Chinese elm. While I was there, several Gulf Fritillaries visited the vine. One female, contentedly sunning herself on the passion flower, was enthusiastically chased away by three aggressive males. A short while later, she began laying her eggs on the supple leaves of the passion flower—a concrete reminder of the butterfly garden's self-rejuvenation.

## SHARING YOUR GARDEN PATCH

Vegetables and herbs also serve as food plants for many caterpillars. Many whites feed on cabbage, broccoli, and collards; the Black Swallowtail enjoys carrot, parsley, dill, and celery; the Alfalfa Butterfly, as its name implies, frequents alfalfa; the Gray Hairstreak likes beans; and the Painted Lady and West Coast Lady feed on mallow as well as other food plants. Most butterfly gardeners find a generous planting is enough to supply both the caterpillars and themselves, but if you want to protect particular plants from being eaten, cover them with netting to deflect egg-laying females, or gather the caterpillars and transfer them to the plants you've reserved for butterflies.

## WILDFLOWER HOSTS

Wildflowers are particular favorites of many butterflies and should be tolerated and even nurtured by butterfly gardeners. For years Hugh Newman battled the head gardener of Winston Churchill's Chartwell estate who wanted to clear the grounds of all nettlebeds. Finally, Newman won approval for a number of nettlebeds. Newman advises, "Usually nothing more than a little neglect is needed in order to establish a nettlebed." He further suggests growing the nettlebed "somewhere by the rubbish heap near the garden shed," where an open door or window might harbor hibernating Peacocks or Small Tortoiseshells. "Then in the spring, when they wake up again and come out to feed, a nettlebed in the sun just round the corner may well seem inviting enough for a female to settle there to lay her large batch of green eggs," Newman hypothesizes.

Other wildflower hosts include lupine, plantain, cresses, pearly everlasting, vetches, sorrel, and dock, which nurse the Common and Silvery Blue, Buckeye, the Sara and Falcate Orangetip, American Painted Lady, the Eastern and Western Tailed Blue, and the American and Purplish Copper respectively. Asters, lupines, violets, thistles, milkweeds, clovers, and carrots are examples of wild food plants that also have cultivated varieties, but sometimes larvae prefer or even require the wild varieties.

As discussed in Chapter Four, wildflowers often have specific habitat requirements, which must be fulfilled in your garden if they are to flourish.

*Passion flower, shown here with Gulf Fritillary larvae and a chrysalis, is a particularly attractive food plant.*

69

The willows, alders, violets, and cranberry which harbor Mourning Cloaks, Green Commas, fritillaries, and Bog Coppers in the naturally moist environment of the Oxen Pond botanical garden "can be grown in the home garden by increasing the soil's capability to retain moisture," says curator Bernard Jackson. He suggests adding moisture-retentive peat moss or leafmold to the soil but stresses that good drainage is also necessary. To create a small bog, place a shallow saucer of plastic sheeting a foot below ground level. Cut a hole in the lowest point of the "bog" for drainage. Then fill the basin with shredded peat. For the dedicated gardener, habitat improvement and maintenance is an ongoing project, he cautions.

But such manipulation of nature's bounty can also benefit a region's butterfly populations. According to Jo Brewer, cudweed, a host plant of the American Painted Lady, grows only two inches high in its natural roadside habitat. But in rich garden soil, the plant will grow as high as four inches and may offer additional sustenance to hungry caterpillars that often overcrowd the tiny roadside plants.

## LAWNS AND WEEDS

"Any plant is a weed if it insists upon growing where the husband-man wants another plant to grow. It is a plant out of place in the eye of man; in the nice eye of nature it is very much in place," writes Edwin Rollin Spencer in *All About Weeds*. "To fail to use a form of nature," he continues, "is to admit defeat at its hands. . . . There is a reason, a utilitarian reason, for loving our enemies. If we are to fight weeds all our lives, it matters not whether we know their names or personalities, but if we are to use them as they should be used, we need to know and to love them." In addition to nitrate enriching and medicinal properties that Spencer attributes to weeds, I would add their aesthetic property as natural butterfly nurseries.

Clover, cudweed, and wild grasses are typical "weeds" that nourish butterfly larvae. Clover is the food plant of both sulphurs and tailed blues and also serves as a nectar source for Tawny Skippers, Gray Hair-streaks, and other species. Cudweed frequently colonizes dichondra lawns and if left alone will itself be colonized by the larvae of the American Painted Lady.

Tall grasses left unmowed and mixed with wildflowers create a natural meadow that is irresistible to butterflies and ideal for the larvae of many species. At the Schlitz Audubon Center in Milwaukee, Wisconsin, an abundance of grasses has sparked an enormous outbreak of the European Skipper, an introduced butterfly which has not become a pest but a valuable aesthetic and interpretive resource.

In contrast, the eradication of acres of tall-grass prairie in the central United States, has depleted the populations of the Smoky Eyed Brown, Regal Fritillary, Dakota Skipper, and Powesheik Skipper which feed on grasses and wildflowers, according to Paul Opler. The preservation of prairie butterflies, says Opler, requires preserves of at least one hundred, and preferably one thousand acres in size. Small reserves or corridors connecting the large conservation areas would aid immigration and colonization, he claims. Butterfly gardens could play an important role in this prairie preserve system.

In fact, many midwestern gardeners are experimenting with native prairie grasses as a substitute for Kentucky bluegrass, because these varieties require no irrigation and nurture a variety of prairie birds, small mammals, and insects. But suburban and urban gardeners should be warned that a spreading garden meadow may irritate neighbors and violate local weed control ordinances. To prevent colonization of neighboring yards, cut off flower heads before they go to seed, and try to place your "hayfield" where it will be least invasive on bordering lawns.

One butterfly gardener I visited had a front-yard meadow dancing with fennel, milkweed, Queen Anne's lace, dandelion, and cultivated varieties including verbena, daisies, gaillardia, geranium, phlox, and violets. Although his neighbors expressed initial concern, he claimed they no longer objected to the unconventional look. "I was gonna have a meadow here, and by George, now I have a meadow," he remarked, surveying the Cabbage Butterflies, West Coast Ladies, Gulf Fritillaries, Marine Blues, and Fiery Skippers flitting over the waving grasses. The same person hospitably provided passion flower, alfalfa, mallow, cabbage, and dill in his backyard vegetable plot as food plants for his winged guests.

As tall grasses and meadow flowers are likely to harbor numerous larvae throughout the butterfly season, the meadow should be mowed only at the end of the butterfly season, and then with special care to avoid especially active larval sites. Miriam Rothschild waits until fall to

*Many food plants serve related butterflies; here the Monarch (left) and Queen (right) utilize milkweed.*

cut her grass, allows a few days after mowing to enable the caterpillars to crawl down into the shorter grass before removing the mulch, and "for the sake of larval butterflies," always leaves some portion of her garden uncut.

## PLANTING AND CARE OF FOOD PLANTS

In planning larval food plants, select appropriate varieties for the particular time of year when their corresponding butterfly species are on the wing. Food plants for early spring butterflies should be started indoors and brought out in pots or transplanted in time to be available for egg-laying females. Enough food plant should be planted for all generations of a particular species, but remember, too, that the complex of variables determining host choice may make your butterflies prefer different food plants from year to year.

Food plants can be placed away from nectar sources or cultivated beds, or scattered among them. Milkweed, thistle, aster, lupine, violets, and everlastings are a showy complement to cultivated ornamental flowers. But nettles might be better hidden behind nectar sources, where the butterflies but not the casual observer will find them. The silvery-gray leaves of everlasting make a beautiful counterpoint to the darker green foliage of other plants, and fennel's thin, lacy leaves and umbrella-shaped flower heads bounce attractively in the shadows of flowering grasses. Like nectar sources, food plants should be planted in dense patches to attract a greater number of butterflies and provide ample nourishment for hungry caterpillars.

Take care to plant food plants in the appropriate habitat for the species which use them as hosts. Some butterflies prefer dappled sunlight or even shade for egg-laying, while others oviposit in direct sunlight. Potted food plants can be conveniently moved to the appropriate exposure and replaced by others when a new species is in season. Entomologist Dr. Rudi Mattoni keeps a number of potted food plants on an east-facing, second-floor balcony at his home, where they receive plenty of sunlight and are readily accessible for his many ongoing experiments.

The borders of gardens adjacent to walls or fences offer protection to egg-laying females. The south-facing stone wall at the Drum Manor Butterfly Garden provides shelter and acts as a sun trap, absorbing and emitting heat which prolongs the growing season of the garden's vegetation. Food plants grown under trellises and canopies also receive protection from birds and rain. The truly industrious gardener may want to build a cage around a patch of food plants, or construct a butterfly house, a subject which will be addressed in Chapter Seven.

Sleeving is a more tedious, but extremely effective way to insure the survival and maturation of a larval population. Fine-mesh netting placed over entire plants or around stems and branches of food plants will protect the eggs, caterpillars, and pupae from birds and spiders. For branches or stems, make a sleeve of netting that is open on both ends. Slip it over the branch and tie it tightly on each end. Empty the sleeve of caterpillar droppings (frass) regularly, by unwinding the string on the low end and tapping the frass out. When most of the leaves on the branch have been eaten, the caterpillars can be moved to an adjacent branch and resleeved. If you want caterpillars to pupate and hatch in these enclosures, make sure they have adequate room to maneuver. Finally, water food plants from below so as not to drown caterpillars, pupae, and eggs. Excessive moisture accumulation may cause infectious bacteria or mold, which can kill larvae.

## EXTENDING YOUR BUTTERFLY GARDEN

Nearby forests, prairies, and even yards can be used to further the success of your butterfly garden. Mourning Cloaks may come to your yard for the nectar of daisies and dogbane, but lay their eggs in the neighbors' boulevard elm. A nearby meadow may provide mustard and buckwheat seeds for your fledgling hayfield, as well as a supply of eggs, larvae, and pupae for you to gather and transplant to your garden. Remember, however, to obtain permission before removing flora or fauna from private or public property, and take care not to disturb rare native species.

Perhaps the most natural and beautiful butterfly gardens are those which manage to erase the boundaries between the altered surroundings of man and the untainted abode of wild creatures. In the canyon near my parents' southern California home, the Western Tiger Swallowtail feeds on California sycamore, the Anise Swallowtail hovers over fennel, the California Sister is nursed by coast live oak, the California Ringlet nestles among the grasses, the Lorquin's Admiral munches willow, and the Cabbage Butterfly flourishes on wild mustard. The Buckeye, Fiery Skipper, Marine Blue, and Funereal Duskywing also visit the canyon. And buckwheat, lupine, and a number of wild grasses have spread to my parents' canyon-facing slope. In their garden, they nurture Felicia daisies, impatiens, marigolds, agapanthus, and other nectar producers that announce an open invitation to the garden's neighboring butterfly colonies. Such a garden, as we will see in the following chapter, can be the location of a thousand captivating observations and pleasurable activities.

S E V E N

# BUTTERFLY GARDEN ACTIVITIES

$\mathbf{B}$utterfly gardening is a participatory as well as an appreciative art. Whether you observe on a casual basis or from a scientific perspective, your study of butterfly variety and life cycle will give you a better understanding and appreciation of the multifaceted butterfly kingdom and perhaps engender some original discoveries. Whatever the extent of your participation, a few pieces of equipment—butterfly net, hand lens, field guide, and notebook—will come in handy and enrich your experiences.

## A BUTTERFLY NET

Even readers with no intention of making a butterfly collection may need a net for identifying butterflies that seldom alight or for capturing egg-laying females for transfer to their food plants. Nets can be purchased from any biological supply house or hobby shop or, for slightly less cost, can be made at home. In either case, a sturdy handle and fine netting through which air passes through easily are essential. Fourth of July butterfly counts conducted by the Xerces Society hold net-building parties in which participants fashion their own nets from inexpensive but good materials. To make your own net, bend a piece of fourteen-gauge galvanized steel wire into a circular shape and bend back both its ends into two-inch lips. Fit a pre-made net (available at a biological supply house) onto the steel rim, and set the lips into either side of a grooved wooden dowel. Then press the dowel snugly into a three-foot-long piece of half-inch PVC piping.

Stalk a butterfly slowly, and quietly, and from behind where it is least likely to see you. A perching butterfly is easiest to capture. When the butterfly settles, move your net swiftly across the plane of the butterfly, and immediately flip the net, trapping the butterfly inside. When the subject is on the ground, clap the net over it and lift the top of the bag so the butterfly flies up inside.

Persistence and concentration are the keys to netting butterflies—qualitites adroitly exhibited by my friend Rudi Mattoni one day on a Malibu mountain road. Spying a Bernardino Blue burst away from a

*Some equipment: net, container, field guide, notebook, hand lens, foreceps, glassine envelopes, and binoculars.*

buckwheat plant and across the road ahead of us, Rudi charged to the site of the target, leading with his long-handled net, swished the net artfully through the air, and without a hitch fell back into step alongside me. Sure enough, the tiny blue, dazed but unharmed, fluttered in the net.

Having captured a butterfly, handle the netting gently, taking care not to damage the fragile creature. Use forceps or tweezers rather than your fingers to hold the butterfly. Robert Michael Pyle suggests stamp tongs, which don't have sharp or serrated edges. Clamp all four wings of your subject at the base with the forceps, making sure the legs are visible, which indicates that the wings are correctly situated over the butterfly's back. A proper hold will keep the butterfly still and prevent the wings from tearing.

To release the butterfly, simply relax your grip on the forceps, allowing the insect to fly away. Butterflies that you intend to take home should be placed in small glassine envelopes (similar to stamp envelopes), which can be purchased at biological supply stores. In the field, keep the envelopes in a cooler (about the same temperature as your refrigerator), which will keep the butterflies still and safe. A Band-Aid box is an ideal container for protecting the fragile butterflies while you travel.

## OPTICS

A hand lens, or strong magnifying glass, is necessary to observe the intricacies of butterfly anatomy. Under the spell of this optical truth serum, a butterfly's eyes become multi-faceted bubbles, the exquisite engineering of its proboscis fascinates and perplexes. A butterfly egg is amplified into a tall, shiny, striated being bursting with butterfly potential, and a caterpillar's working mandibles become an efficient miniature eating machine. A pair of binoculars inverted magnifies just like a hand lens. Used in the usual way, binoculars allow you to observe distant butterflies going about their usual business and to spot fleeting butterflies more frequently in the field.

## FIELD GUIDES

Butterfly field guides are available which cover North America, various states, or specific regions. To locate the one most suitable for your purposes, consult the bibliography of this book, and contact bookstores, museums, or butterfly clubs in your area. A good field guide is an unequaled resource for the butterfly gardener who wishes to identify a variety of species or a particular subspecies that occurs only in a defined area. Some field guides use arrows to point out field marks, or distinctive markings which distinguish similar species or the sexes of a single species. The field marks system, developed by Roger Tory Peterson, is a valuable asset when trying to tell the Lorquin's Admiral from the California Sister, for instance. A field guide is also an entertaining source of interesting butterfly natural history, and a helpful indicator of life-cycle characteristics and behavior.

## THE FIELD NOTEBOOK

An accurate and thorough record of the observations you make while studying butterflies, whether as a garden spectator or butterfly house researcher, will provide an absorbing diary of your butterfly experiences and important documentation of any incidental discoveries. Notes should be recorded immediately after observation, so that, for example, an orange butterfly with a yellow sheen is not described as a yellow butterfly with an orange sheen.

A field notebook is particularly important for those who rear butterflies. Caterpillar behavior should be recorded daily, hourly, and sometimes even minute to minute depending on what you are trying to discover. Time between moltings; response to light, darkness, heat, wind, and touch; the lifetime of food plants placed in water; the time it takes various species of caterpillars to consume their food plants; and the total time it takes to raise larvae to adulthood are all valuable observations you may want to record.

In the garden, you might want to record the time, date, location, sex, and abundance of species you spot on the various vegetation. The former Curator of Insects at the American Museum of Natural History, Frank Lutz, once made a bargain with the museum's director in which they agreed that beginning with the 501st species of insect Lutz found in his suburban New York lot, he would receive a salary increase of ten dollars per additional species. The bet was never made official, but Lutz began counting . . . and counting . . . and counting—and recording. Eventually he tabulated 1402 species, including 35 species of butterflies among which were the Great Spangled Fritillary, Pearly Crescentspot,

Baltimore, Question Mark, Mourning Cloak, Red Admiral, American Painted Lady, Buckeye, Red-spotted Purple, Viceroy, Gray Hairstreak, Spring Azure, Cabbage Butterfly, Common Sulphur, Eastern Black Swallowtail, Spicebush Swallowtail, and Tiger Swallowtail. "My salary has not been increased," writes Lutz in the book his research fostered, "but I have had a lot of fun. So can you."

Not only can you have a lot of fun, you can strengthen the attraction of your garden to butterflies by discovering and recording their preferences and actually contribute to the scientists' and laymen's understanding of the butterfly kingdom. Your observations can be shared with neighbors, local butterfly gardeners, or even with the readers of entomological journals or newsletters—spreading your experience far beyond the walls of your butterfly garden.

## EXPERIMENTS

Elaborate experiments, conducted with care and persistence, are a particularly effective way to find out which plants grow best in your garden and which butterflies are most attracted to the habitats you've provided.

When performing an experiment, use a scientific approach involving a control group which varies from the group you are testing in only one way. Conditions such as caterpillar age; temperature, humidity, and sun exposure in the test site; and food plant condition should all be considered. Complete the experiment several times on different subjects to test the reliability of your results. An average of several test-runs should enable you to make an informed conclusion.

A site-management experiment on the introduction of a species that inhabits the region but has not yet become established in your yard would be particularly interesting. Would the twenty or thirty Anise Swallowtail larvae you bring to the fennel plants in your garden survive? How many would mature to adulthood? Would the adult butterflies remain and reproduce in their new habitat? What would be the effect of a violent thunderstorm or a flock of migrating birds on the population? A study on territoriality might reveal that a certain kind of perching post would attract more male butterflies to your garden. As a boy, Robert Michael Pyle noticed that male Hackberry Butterflies habitually perched on a Chinese elm in his backyard rather than on the hackberry tree down the block. The males did travel to the hackberry tree to court receptive females, but continually returned to the Chinese elm, where the females never ventured. Such an observation might be the impetus for planting another Chinese elm or, possibly, a nearby hackberry tree.

Quantitative and qualitative information culled from your experiments and observations can be compared from year to year for a chronological, descriptive record. Such information would be valuable to your local natural history museum or entomology club as the first installment in a regional butterfly "data bank." You might even compete, as birdwatchers do, with fellow butterfly gardeners to see who can sight and identify the greatest numbers of species.

Creating a butterfly collection, though not a recommended *garden* activity, is also an informative and valuable endeavor. As only a relatively few specimens are collected and mounted, butterfly populations suffer minimally, unless the particular species is extremely rare or local. Techniques for capturing, preserving, and mounting butterflies can be learned from many field guides or from local museum curators or entomologists. Collections document, among other things, where each species appears and how size, markings, coloration, and other anatomical characteristics are affected by genetic or environmental factors. They may also serve as an educational tool to stimulate the conservation and study of butterflies. Children are particularly fascinated with butterfly collections and may engage in this activity as a first step toward a lifelong interest in biology.

## CHILDREN AND BUTTERFLIES

An active butterfly garden can also be a learning environment for children. A butterfly garden in the school yard could serve as an outdoor insect laboratory for students studying the life cycle, habits, and classification of insects including butterflies. For younger children, games could be devised around the butterfly theme. Adoption papers listing a butterfly's species, sex, and physical description could be made out. Butterfly kite construction would make a colorful and fun rainy-day craft. Games with children imitating butterfly flight patterns or racing to their food plants or nectar sources could be originated. Caterpillar races would be most entertaining, and a butterfly Halloween costume would certainly add levity to an otherwise frightening repertoire.

## PHOTOGRAPHY

Photographing butterflies, whether in the wild or in a controlled environment like a butterfly house, is an ideal substitute for collecting. As with any easily frightened subject, photographing an unpredictable butterfly is quite a challenge, but one that is reduced by the increasing availability of sophisticated photographic equipment for close-up picture taking. A telephoto with bellows, or macro lens between 100 and 300 millimeters will be necessary for even slightly distant subjects. When photographing butterflies in trees or high bushes, take care to adjust for the increase in sunlight. Additional information on close-up photography is available in many photography books or from your local camera dealer.

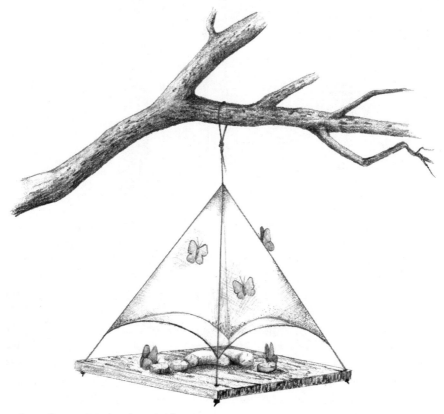

*A butterfly trap baited with rotting bananas.*

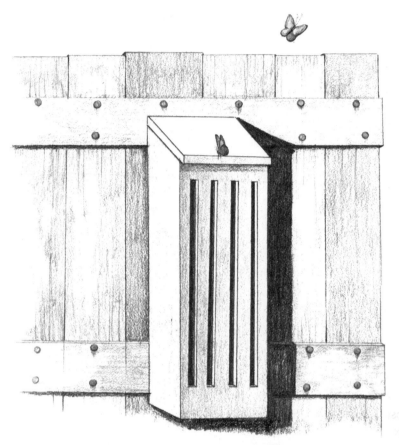

*Warm winter days will sometimes draw butterflies out of garden hibernation boxes.*

## BUTTERFLY ENCLOSURES

Photographing and studying butterflies is less difficult if the insects are confined, though not harmed, in a butterfly trap or house. A trap, consisting of a baited platform covered by a fine netting, is also useful for counting and gathering a number of butterflies. To make a trap, suspend a two-foot-square piece of netting (or a butterfly net) about six inches above a platform or tray, either by hanging the tray from the four corners of the netting, or mounting the netting on poles surrounding the tray. When the platform or tray is baited with rotting fruit, nectar blossoms, or other treats, butterflies will alight on the platform; as they naturally take to the air in a vertical direction, they will not be able to escape.

Jo Brewer has successfully caught Question Marks, Commas, Mourning Cloaks, Red-spotted Purples, and many moths in her cylindrical hanging traps baited with beer, bananas, brown sugar, and yeast. One day, she even trapped fifty-three Red Admirals! Jennifer and Denis Owen of Leicester, England have trapped numerous butterflies in their tailored, tent-like Malaise trap. The Owens frequently mark and release their trapped butterflies and have discovered that most do not return to the garden, leading them to believe that suburban gardens attract a mobile community of butterflies.

## HIBERNATION BOXES

Hibernation boxes, as the name implies, provide an artificial enclosure which encourages the butterflies in your garden to remain through the cold months. A hibernation box consists of a tall narrow hollow box, with open slits in the front. Butterflies can crawl through the slits and cling to the inside of the box through the winter. To make one, build a four-foot-high and approximately six-inch-square box of unplaned, unpainted wood. Cut one-half by three-inch (or larger) vertical slots in the front of the box, and fashion a hinged door for the top of the box. Ideally, line the inside of the box with rough bark or a similar substrate to allow butterflies the best gripping surface. Then, mount the box so that the bottom is about five feet above the ground. Mounted tin cans, unoccupied birdhouses, and, as Hugh Newman discovered, garden sheds, though less protected from birds and other predators, also act as hibernation shelters.

Place hibernation boxes near the host plants of hibernating species, so that the newly active spring butterflies will more likely lay eggs in your garden. Hibernation boxes are especially valuable for northern gardeners who may want to invite the Compton Tortoiseshell or Gray Comma to stay the winter. Hibernating guests can be watched and counted by opening the hinged top of the box. And your efforts may one day be rewarded by the surprising emergence of a drowsy lepidopteran into the warm winter sun. Should this occur, sugar-water or home-grown blossoms will keep it busy until it retreats once again, as the evening cools, into the shelter of its cozy box.

## BUTTERFLY HOUSES

Butterfly houses provide a controlled environment for the study and breeding of butterflies without the hazards of predation and weather. They range in size from a cage of mesh covering a baby's playpen to a greenhouse complete with heating and ventilation systems, artificial light, and mist sprayers to simulate humidity. Hugh Newman recommends a cage made of mosquito netting attached to a number of movable stakes surrounding whatever nectar source is blooming at the time. Jo Brewer uses a large, boxlike camping tent for rearing and observation. The New York Zoological Society scientists in Trinidad initially housed their study subjects in a nine-foot-high enclosure called Flutter Inn. This structure was later replaced by an aluminum-framed bungalow standing directly adjacent to the team's own living quarters. Whichever you choose, the enclosure should be wind resistant, large enough to allow room for short flights, and, of course, well stocked with nectar or other nourishment sources for imagoes and food plants for growing caterpillars.

## BUTTERFLY HOUSES AROUND THE WORLD

Though few and scattered, the world's public butterfly houses attract a great many intrigued visitors. The London Butterfly House in Syon Park is a ten thousand-square-foot glass greenhouse containing hundreds of native and exotic butterflies. Chinese painted quail, which are reluctant flyers, roam between the ponds and the waterfalls eating predatory spiders and ants. The larvae of the South American Owl Butterfly, tropical swallowtails, and Golden Birdwing feast on banana trees, citrus, and *Aristolochia* vines. And a whole host of other fluttering rainbows nectar on lantana, buddleia, hoya, African marigold, and a potion of fruit, honey, and rum. The proprietor, Clive Farrell, has recently opened butterfly houses in Edinburgh, Weymouth, and Stratford-on-Avon.

Also in England, Worldwide Butterflies runs a butterfly house in a fifty-room mansion in Sherborne filled with tropical plants and exotic butterflies. Proprietor Robert Goodden breeds and sells butterflies to students, couples who want to release them at weddings, and producers of television commercials and movies. The same group also operates the Lullingstone Silk Farm which has been commissioned to produce silk for royal garments.

*A butterfly house, containing: nectar sources and larval food plants (potted or in soil), rearing containers, and butterflies.*

Tokyo's Tama Zoological Park features a butterfly hot house where the Japanese Blue Monarch, Small White Butterfly, and five swallowtail species, among others, mature and reproduce before enthralled visitors. At least 50 of Sri Lanka's 242 butterfly species live in the Dehiwela Zoological Gardens' eighth-of-an-acre greenhouse. A $450,000 butterfly house for 365 species is being constructed in Australia's Melbourne Zoo.

And the U.S., too, may soon join the roster of countries with large public butterfly houses. The National Zoo in Washington, D.C. plans to develop a national butterfly center complete with both a butterfly house and garden. The New York Zoological Society is considering a similar facility.

EIGHT

# HOW TO REAR BUTTERFLIES

Rearing butterflies, an absorbing activity for the butterfly gardener cum amateur entomologist, can increase the abundance of butterflies in your garden and be a rewarding experience in itself. Rearing stock can be obtained from the wild in any stage of the life cycle or from biological supply houses.

## OBTAINING EGGS

To obtain eggs in the wild, either gather them after a female has laid them or search for them on the food plant favorite of a particular species. Do not remove the eggs from the leaves on which they have been laid. Rather, gather the stems or even the entire branch holding the eggs and take them to your garden. Then place the stems in water where they should remain fresh for a week or so until the eggs hatch; the same stems will provide the first food plant for the newly hatched caterpillars.

Eggs can also be obtained by capturing a female and keeping her in a cage with potted or cut food plant until she lays her eggs. Since females mate very shortly after emergence, the female you catch is likely to already have mated and will then lay her fertile eggs within a few days. Nectar blossoms or a paper towel saturated with sugar- or honey-water should be provided for the ovipositing female.

## CATERPILLARS

Learn which food plants and caterpillars are indigenous to your region. Holes in leaves often give away the presence of caterpillars. Remember to look on the undersides of leaves, as this is where caterpillars usually rest. Larvae, like eggs, will be far safer in your home than in the wild, and rearing them may bolster an adult population of a particular species in your neighborhood. This fact was rudely brought home to me one day while I was vigorously collecting Gulf Fritillary larvae from a passion flower vine. With my bag nearly full of late instar larvae—which would pupate within a matter of days, but were still not as many as I had hoped to collect—I returned to the site of an early instar caterpillar I had earlier passed over. Suddenly there was a lightning-fast movement toward the caterpillar, and then the tiny victim was simply gone. Whatever had grabbed it had been so fast that I only saw a blur—a harsh reminder of caterpillar vulnerability.

## PUPAE

Although butterflies' well-camouflaged chrysalises are extremely hard to find, the eagle-eyed observer will sometimes find them on the stems of food plants, attached to walls, fences, logs, or trees, or under the eaves of a house. The color of a species' chrysalis may provide a clue to the backgrounds against which it will pupate. Robert Wuttken, a Santa Monica butterfly gardener, reports that the Anise Swallowtails which feed on his fennel plants like to pupate on a nearby weather-beaten wood fence, against which the brown chrysalises are almost indistinguishable.

When gathering either pupae, caterpillars, or eggs, take the opportunity to learn the life-stage characteristics of various species. The Mourning Cloak, Compton Tortoiseshell, Baltimore, and checkerspots lay their eggs in clusters and, as larvae, feed communally. The Viceroy and other admirals overwinter in hibernaculi constructed from food plant leaves and silk. Because swallowtail larvae feed individually they may appear quite suddenly on a food plant which you have repeatedly inspected and even given up on.

## COMMERCIAL SUPPLIERS

A number of suppliers sell eggs, larvae, and pupae to school groups, scientists, photographers, collectors, and other individuals. Insect Lore Products in California produces a "Butterfly Garden" rearing kit containing Painted Lady and Buckeye larvae that also comes in a classroom version. Breeder of Lepidoptera John Staples, in Rochester, New York, sells Eastern Black Swallowtail, Red Admiral, Orange Sulphur, and Common Sulphur eggs by the dozen or the hundred; Spicebush Swallowtail pupae individually or by the dozen; and several species of moth eggs and pupae. Such purchased stock, if the species is also indigenous to your region, should adapt well to your garden.

## REARING CONTAINERS

Rearing containers vary from the simple jam jar with holes punched in the top to customized kennel-sized cages. Many standard containers—aquariums, cardboard boxes, jars—can be improvised for rearing cages, or you can design and build your own. In any case, several criteria should be met. A tight lid or fine netting will prevent wandering caterpillars from escaping. The cage should be well ventilated to prevent disease-causing mold and bacteria from growing. Direct sunlight may be too warm for eggs, caterpillars, and pupae, but short spells of sunlight will help the newly emerged butterflies to dry and pump up their wings. A rough surface from which pupae can hang is also necessary. And make certain that there is enough room for the young imagoes to spread their wings.

Clear plastic boxes about the size of a shoe box can be used to house a few caterpillars. The Cabbage Butterfly and many other species can pupate right on the smooth sides, but many species will need a rougher surface. Line the bottom of the box with slightly damp paper toweling which will create enough humidity to keep the caterpillars from drying out and be easily removable for cleaning. Using a heated nail, punch holes in each side of the box for ventilation, and cover them with fine mesh. More ventilation will be created as you replace the old food plant with new.

A large potted food plant or window box covered with netting supported by a frame also works well as a rearing cage. Simply place a branch in the pot, drape the netting over the branch, and fasten the netting securely to the sides of the pot with a rubber band or string. Wire stretched over window boxes to form a dome and covered with netting works just as well. Californian Tony Leigh's self-made rearing cage consists of two eight-inch cake tins and a twelve-inch-wide section of window screening. After wrapping the screening into a cylinder and stapling it securely, he places one cake tin underneath it and one on top—a setup which makes his caterpillars both accessible and easy to see.

Cardboard boxes can be variously manipulated to create rearing cages. In my apartment, I raise caterpillars in a small square cardboard

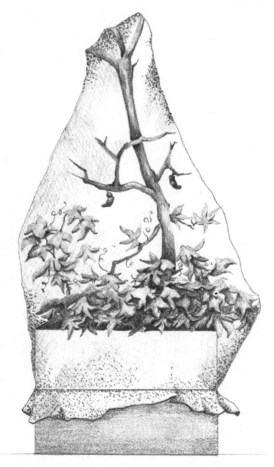

*A rearing set-up, including cut food plant, a stick for pupating caterpillars, and protective netting.*

box containing two glass jars. The lid of one jar is pierced with holes for food plant stems; the jar is filled with water to keep the food plant fresh. The other contains a branch packed in dirt, which supports a net covering and provides a pupating surface. The netting is secured around the box with a rubber band. Tom Dimock goes one step further and cuts away all but the margins of the sides and top of a cardboard box, leaving a simple cardboard frame. He covers the openings with fine nylon mesh, allowing him to see the active caterpillars from any perspective. On one side of the box, he fashions a hinged doorway for removing frass and replacing food plant.

Dimock also uses a larger cage (approximately two by two by four feet) for rearing large broods. When I visited him, there were half a dozen Red Admirals flying among the nettle plants inside. Large and small cages can also be purchased from biological supply houses.

## CATERPILLAR CARE

Though by nature hardy, independent creatures, caterpillars need proper attention and care. A constant supply of fresh food plants—young tender leaves for young caterpillars, a combination of young and mature leaves for older larvae—will keep your brood from starving or pupating prematurely because they run short of food. Hungry older caterpillars may consume more than you expect, so a back-up food source may come in handy. Avoid using plants from busy roadsides that may be contaminated by car exhaust or ones that have been sprayed with insecticide or herbicide. Let plants that need rinsing dry before feeding them to caterpillars. One night, having gone out to a roadside patch of fennel for my hungry charges, I was surprised to discover the familiar black and white blotch of an early instar Anise Swallowtail caterpillar. Searching the rest of the leaves, I found two more young larvae. The trio, which I took home to raise with my other caterpillars, was a rewarding sidelight to what had begun as a simple trip to the "grocery."

Food plants should be replaced at least once a week, though some will wilt within a day and others will last as long as two weeks. Packing damp soil or sand around cut food plants will often keep them longer than water. Extra food plants can be kept fresh in tightly closed plastic bags in the refrigerator, or in jars of water, covered with plastic, and

*A joyful moment—releasing a newly-hatched Checkered White.*

stored in the refrigerator. Cut food plants at an angle with a razor blade or sharp scissors for maximum water absorption.

When changing the food plant, avoid handling the caterpillars excessively. Children will particularly enjoy the cool varied texture of larval skin and hair, but should be instructed to handle gently. Tiny caterpillars can be moved by allowing them to crawl onto a small paint brush and then off again onto the new food plant. When using cut food plants in water, cover any open areas around stems into which caterpillars might fall and drown.

Do not disturb a caterpillar that is beginning to molt, as it is attached to the leaf with silk. The silk holds its old skin in place while it works to get free from it. If moved, it may not escape from the old skin and will die. Newly molted larvae are extremely fragile and should not be handled or bumped.

91

Also place some food plant flush with the bottom and sides of your container, so that wanderers will find ample food. Caterpillars that are ready to pupate are particularly prone to wandering and will need to be watched, lest they escape. A Gulf Fritillary larva once found its way three-quarters of the way up my wall where it was just about to spin its silk pupating pad when I found it! A rough surface like a branch or a piece of bark should be provided for pupating larvae.

## CHRYSALIS CARE

Chrysalises are extremely fragile and should not be handled frequently or roughly. In areas of low humidity, pupae should be sprayed weekly with a fine mist. Collected in the wild, they should be taken with their stems or the strip of bark to which they are attached and kept carefully in the same position in which they are hanging. If the pupa is attached to an immovable surface like a fence or house, slice the silk pad with a razor blade close to the point of attachment or slowly and gently twist the pupa off the silk pad (taking care not to squeeze the pupa out of shape). Then attach the pupa to a piece of cardboard or bark, with a tiny drop of glue or, if there is a strand of silk protruding, with a piece of tape. Swallowtails attach themselves with a silken girdle as well as a silk pad. The girdle can be replaced with a loop of thread and taped to a new surface, keeping the pupa at the same angle at which you found it.

A butterfly rearer's pupa-handling skills will sooner or later be put to the test, as mine once were when my desire to photograph two Monarch pupae on the branch I had provided in my rearing cage forced me to remove the net covering on which a third larva had unpredictably pupated. As I lifted the netting to remove the chrysalis, it caught on the branch, causing the chrysalis to fall. Fortunately, the unraveling silk pad caught on a protrusion and broke the pupa's fall. After cutting away the excess silk, I attached the chrysalis to a piece of cardboard with tape and laid the cardboard over a small box. Four days later, to my relief and satisfaction, a healthy Monarch butterfly emerged into adulthood. The box I transferred my Monarch to is called an emerging cage and is often a convenient way to separate adults from caterpillars and to insure that imagoes have enough room to spread their wings.

*To coax a butterfly to sip from blossoms or sugarwater, hold it firmly with forceps and gently unwind its proboscis with a toothpick.*

## CARE OF CAPTIVE FEMALES

Females bred from eggs in your cage or captured in the wild to produce eggs for rearing need fresh nectar blossoms or a solution of sugar- or honey-water. Egg-laying females should be watched closely and released when they have laid the number of eggs you desire. Cut blossoms should be changed daily, as they produce a limited amount of nectar. A sugar solution will become more concentrated as it evaporates, and therefore, should be monitored to maintain a mixture dilute enough for the butterflies' sensitive proboscises.

A petri dish or plastic lid filled with paper toweling, cotton, or unscented tissue paper saturated (but not too soggy) with solution is particularly attractive to butterflies, because they can walk on the pad as well as drink from it. Tom Dimock elevates the feeding dish on a pedestal, which gives the dish greater sun exposure and simulates the butterflies' natural above-the-ground flight area. He also places moistened tissue paper on top of the cage netting; butterflies cling to the underside of the netting and sip from the sweet surface.

If a butterfly does not nectar on its own, its appetite may be stimulated by placing its tarsi on the solution-saturated padding. Jocelyn Crane perks up butterflies that are undergoing post-capture shock with a three-foot-long wand affixed with lantana blossoms. A bit of honey on the blossom, slid under the butterfly's proboscis, is like "a piece of chocolate cake offered to a small boy in the dumps," she comments. As a last resort, hold the butterfly firmly with a forceps and carefully unroll its proboscis with a toothpick. After a brief struggle, the butterfly will usually begin to sip the close-at-hand nectar. A Gulf Fritillary with a damaged wing, which spent six weeks crawling from its box, frequently required assisted feedings when it was reluctant to feed itself from the cut blossoms and sugar-water I provided.

## REARING TIMETABLES

The metamorphosis of a butterfly is naturally regulated by and intertwined with the turning of the seasons. Consequently, the butterfly rearer must be familiar with the overwintering habits of the species he raises and the ways in which seasonal changes can be simulated to prompt hibernation and emergence.

In mild climates, caterpillars often overwinter in a substrate of dead leaves or other debris. The Baltimore and many skippers, for instance, spend the cold months in tiny leaf shelters, but crumpled paper toweling will suffice for a cage lining. In many cases these species require a freeze to break diapause. A freeze can be simulated by placing the larvae in a container in the refrigerator for about eight weeks. In cold climates, caterpillars should not be left to overwinter in an outdoor cage, but should be refrigerated until the air warms up. Never put caterpillars or butterflies in any life stage into the freezer.

Butterflies that overwinter as chrysalises, such as swallowtails, should not be allowed to hatch in winter unless you intend to nurture them indoors with sweetened solution or potted nectar sources. Instead, store the pupae in a cool spot, like the garage or potting shed. Spray them regularly with a fine mist and, when the weather warms, open the door so that the newly emerged butterflies can escape and find nectar sources.

The full-grown individuals of species that hibernate as adults can be released even in winter, or may be allowed to hibernate in your attic or garage. Of course, if you tend an indoor butterfly house, you can raise brood after brood throughout the year.

In some cases, you may want to refrigerate pupae. Most of a brood of swallowtails will emerge the first spring after hibernation; the remainder will rest silent and still until the next spring. Staggered emergence times reduce the possibility of total population destruction due to drought or other natural disaster. But a simulated combination of day-

94

length and winter (refrigeration) may fool the butterflies' instinctive timetable and prompt them to emerge sooner than they would naturally.

Tony Leigh placed a number of Indra Swallowtail pupae which did not hatch with the rest of their brood, in the refrigerator for a month. Ten days after removing them to a bed of damp paper toweling and misting them twice a day, they began to hatch. Apparently his care seemed to the butterflies to be a second cold winter, spring's warmth, and the soft spring rains.

## FROM REARING TO BREEDING

The leap from rearing caterpillars to mating adult butterflies is short and exciting. A male and a female reared in suitable rearing cage conditions and left together will likely mate. With ample sunlight, nectar sources, and food plant available, the female will lay her eggs right in the cage.

Tom Dimock goes to elaborate means to make sure his Gulf Fritillaries mate. Observation and experimentation have taught Dimock that sunlight, a light breeze, and temperatures between 75 and 80° Fahrenheit are perfect conditions for butterfly mating. With this in mind, he takes mating pairs in boxes to work with him. At lunchtime, he places the boxes on the front seat of his car, opens the car windows, and waits for the grand event. Particularly reluctant butterflies can be hand-paired, a procedure described as follows in Robert Michael Pyle's Handbook: "Holding each partner in one hand with tweezers, place their abdomens gently together and stroke them back and forth softly. As the male's claspers spread apart, insert the female's rear with very little pressure."

Captive breeding is the ideal environment for controlled, ongoing experiments, and allows genetic characteristics to be studied over several generations. Dimock once bred seven generations of Gulf Fritillaries by mating light and dark colored descendents of a single female with others of similar coloring. The last generations displayed two dissimilar phenotypes—one with a nearly all black upperside, the other with a uniform orange one—in striking contrast to the original female which had a normal orange upperside with regular black markings.

Rearing and breeding also allows you the ultimate satisfaction of watching your charges fly freely into the wild. Whether, like Arlene

Hoffman, you release a brood of majestic Monarchs from a Manhattan office complex or set a flock of fritillaries free above your blossoming verbena, the sheer joy of it will bring home to you once again the pleasures of butterfly gardening.

# CONSERVATION OF BUTTERFLIES

Robert Michael Pyle calls the decline of not only endangered species, but of local butterfly populations in areas inhabited by man the "extinction of experience." "Suppose a creature dies out within your 'radius of reach'—the area to which you have easy access," he explains. "In some respects, it might as well be gone altogether, because you will not be able to see it as you could before." Such extinction of experience makes people more isolated from and less caring of nature, says Pyle, but "the retention of wildlife in the cities and suburbs goes a long way toward maintaining the essential bond between people and nature that breeds a sense of stewardship and responsibility for the land and its life far beyond city limits."

Butterfly gardens, as we have seen, increase habitat availability for butterflies and inspire the relationship between nature and man which can only work for the benefit of both humans and butterflies. Still, the pressures of habitat destruction, pollution, and, to a lesser degree, commercial harvesting, continue to threaten many butterfly populations. "Once almost entirely neglected in favor of larger, furrier animals, butterflies and other beneficial insects under threat have gained much attention lately," comments Pyle. "This change of attitude is coming none too quickly, and it is not at all certain that it has come in time. We are beginning to realize that, without great care, we could lose much of the world's precious butterfly resource."

## CAUSES OF BUTTERFLY DECLINE

Natural disasters like drought, wildfire, prolonged hot or cold spells, and flood, affecting either butterflies or their food plants, can wipe out entire butterfly colonies. Collection and commercial distribution also deplete butterfly populations, but except where a species is extremely rare or local, experts agree that these activities have a minimal impact on a prolific insect. In Taiwan, where millions of butterflies are collected annually to supply the worldwide market for butterfly-adorned objects, butterfly populations rebound. Frequently, commercial ventures contribute to butterfly conservation. Project Papillon uses vacated tomato greenhouses on the British Channel Island of Guernsey to raise butterflies for export. In addition to selling butterflies and drawing tourists to the island, the group is providing several thousand butterflies for reintroduction in Hampstead Heath, where they have become scarce. In Papua New Guinea, the rarest of the large and colorful birdwing butterflies are protected insects; butterfly farmers rear the common species, returning as many to the wild as they sell.

In the developing countries of the butterfly-rich tropics, the most serious threat to butterfly populations is the destruction of their natural forest habitats. The draining of wetlands, development of land for urbanization, and conversion of open country to agricultural monocultures can decimate species with narrow ranges, and kill entire colonies of wide-ranging species. The unregulated use of herbicides on roadsides and other areas further damages the habitat corridors traveled by wide-ranging species. Already urban expansion has led to the extinction of the San Francisco Peninsula's Xerces Blue, and habitat destruction is responsible for the inclusion of ten other butterflies on the U.S. Endangered Species List.

## HABITAT PROTECTION

The protection and addition of habitat areas suitable for butterflies is, therefore, the primary butterfly conservation approach. Your garden can serve as a valuable habitat resource. Rearing and releasing butterflies may also augment populations, as an egg nurtured in your home is more likely to survive to adulthood than one in the wild. With few exceptions—the Cabbage Butterfly and the Orange Sulphur among them—

*The migratory Monarch spends the winter clinging to trees on the California coast and in Mexico. Tragically, these sites are threatened by development and lumbering, respectively.*

butterfly species do not adapt well to human environments. So your efforts to nurse a natural island within the sea of urban expansion, particularly on the behalf of any rare local species, can encourage their ongoing prosperity.

Persuading local officials to cut roadsides in late summer rather than spraying them in spring would also protect an important butterfly habitat. Planted areas could be trimmed when the butterflies have completed their life cycle, insuring also that abundant new growth will be available for a later generation of caterpillars. Abandoned railway lines provide ideal butterfly habitats. Abundant with wildflowers, they make excellent nature trails for hikers and butterfly watchers as well as overflowing nectar corridors for butterflies.

Botanical gardens are another habitat that deserve protection in a butterfly conservation program. According to Bernard Jackson, butterflies in botanical gardens help maintain the area's Lepidoptera gene pool, pollinate vegetation so that seeds can be collected, enrich interpretive programs, and attract photographers, naturalists, and tourists with a flourish of color and movement.

## GARDEN CLUBS

Garden club members are among the foremost butterfly conservationists. According to Eve A. Hannahs, chairman of Butterfly Conservation and Preservation for the National Council of State Garden Clubs (NCSGC) overseeing more than ten thousand member clubs, members cultivate butterfly gardens in city parks and botanical gardens, on roadsides, school grounds, club properties, historical sites, hospital grounds, and even at a state prison. The groups also conduct workshops and nature walks about butterflies, display exhibits, and write articles about butterflies for state and national publications. The Florida Federation of Garden Clubs has begun a sponsorship program for threatened butterflies. Garden club members sponsoring the endangered Schaus' Swallowtail have planted acres of torchwood, the butterfly's food plants, and plan to introduce the butterfly into this habitat.

In cooperation with the Federal Highway Administration and state highway administrations, NCSGC has founded Operation Wildflower, to promote the proliferation of wildflowers along federal highways. With the garden clubs' guidance and seed contributions, federal crews plant and maintain roadside butterfly gardens. In addition to providing seasonal color and insect preserves, the project enhances erosion control and reduces landscaping and road maintenance costs.

Other groups also advocate wildflower propagation and, hence, the conservation of butterflies. The New England Wild Flower Society and the Soil Conservation Society of America each produce a list of regional native plant and wildflower nurseries. Author of *The Woman's Day Book of Wildflowers*, Jean Hersey, reports that Texas highway crews delay mowing each year until the seeds of wildflowers have fallen. Miles of bluebonnets, passion flower, gaillardia, red clover, and sunflower—valuable butterfly nectar and food sources—line the state's highways. In Georgia, adds Hersey, the highway department removed a stand of birdfoot violet before grading a slope, and replaced the flowers when the grading was complete.

## WILDLIFE GROUPS AND ENTOMOLOGICAL SOCIETIES

The Backyard Wildlife Program sponsored by the National Wildlife Federation designates thousands of residential yards as miniature wildlife refuges. The federation distributes a kit to teach residents how to create such a refuge, including mention of butterfly requirements, and makes available a list of other residents in each state who have joined the program. The Massachusetts Audubon Society cultivates a butterfly garden at its Endicott Regional Center in Wenham. And the Palos Verdes Peninsula Audubon Society conducts a local butterfly count as part of the Xerces Society's national Fourth of July Butterfly Count.

Local entomological societies, often operating out of natural history museums, provide valuable information about butterflies and threatened species. The Lorquin Entomological Society in Los Angeles, for instance, recently reported that the southern Florida Atala butterfly, believed to be extinct, can now be observed in several locations near Miami.

The Xerces Society is an international conservation organization dedicated to the protection of rare and endangered butterflies and other invertebrates and their habitats. Each year, the society coordinates a tabulation of different species and the number of butterflies of each species seen by groups across the country on or around the Fourth of July. Compiled and compared from year to year, these data help identify butterfly population trends and problem habitats. The society also provides self-help sheets with instructions on creating, organizing, and managing community butterfly reserves, as well as other topics. Xerces works closely with garden clubs to prepare and distribute regional butterfly gardening information packets.

## THE BUTTERFLY BLUES

In addition to the ten butterfly species that already occupy the U.S. Endangered Species list, thiry-one other butterfly species have been proposed for protected status. This figure gives an indication of the problems faced by uncommon butterfly species.

The El Segundo Blue, listed as an endangered species since 1976, lives only in certain coastal locations in Southern California. Once ranging over thirty-six square miles, the butterfly is now found only on two different sites. On the smaller of these sites, several concerned organizations have worked to remove an introduced ice plant that was competing with the butterfly's buckwheat food plant, and have arranged for additional buckwheat to be planted. The El Segundo Blue population on that site is now increasing. While the fate of the larger site remains undecided, high level negotiations are underway to preserve at least its central area.

When the Palos Verdes Blue was designated as an endangered species in 1980, the few locoweed patches where it was known to feed were given federal protection as critical habitats. But in 1983, a baseball diamond was built on a section of the butterfly's most populated habitat, and the following spring two other locoweed patches were destroyed. Although sightings were common in 1981, no more than half a dozen

*The Atala butterfly, thought to be extinct, has made a comeback recently.*

*Wildflowers planted along roadsides support communities of butterflies.*

Palos Verdes Blues were seen in 1983, and in 1984 and 1985, no sightings whatsoever were made during its February and March flying season. If the Palos Verdes Blue has become extinct, it would be the first time one of the 286 species protected by the Endangered Species Act has become extinct.

Efforts to preserve other species have been more auspicious. Conservationists and developers in Albany, New York have worked together to prevent the destruction of the Karner pine bush, habitat of the Karner Blue. As development reduced this sandy pine barrens to a fraction of its former size, the Xerces Society and other groups moved to persuade local and state authorities to establish a sixty-five hectare reserve for the Karner Blue and other rare species indigenous to the area. Subsequently a study revealed the need for a larger reserve and as conservation efforts increased, compromise flourished. Nearly a thousand acres of Karner pine bush now lie in protected public ownership. Conservation Officer Don Rittner, who has followed the course of the debate, estimates that 100,000 Karner Blues now survive on the Albany City Reserve.

A city ordinance in Pacific Grove, California, where thousands of Monarchs winter annually, makes it "unlawful for any person to molest or interfere with in any way the peaceful occupancy of the Monarch Butterflies." Nevertheless, development continues to impinge on the

*103*

Monarch. The Xerces Society's Monarch Project, promoting the alternative income available from tourism on Monarch preserves, is taking steps to halt development in Californian Monarch groves and restrict lumbering in the butterfly's Mexican overwintering sites.

## WHY PROTECT BUTTERFLIES

Like the California condor, whooping crane, and grizzly bear, butterflies deserve protection. Unlike the relatively few insect pests, butterflies benefit agricultural and botanical efforts by pollinating flowers. As prey for other insects, rodents, and birds, butterflies play an important role in the foodchain. They also contribute to medical and biological research on hereditary characteristics and provide scientists with opportunities to study insect variation, fertility, population dynamics, and evolution. Finally, as every butterfly gardener knows, they provide a unique aesthetic resource. The extinction of the Xerces Blue represents the loss of one tile in the mosaic of butterfly variety, but the remainder of the unimaginably rich artwork need not become a shameful passage in the pages of evolution.

In fact, because many butterflies inhabit such limited ranges, they serve as sensitive ecological indicators, revealing the health or ills of the habitats in which they live, and thus of their fellow inhabitants. Ironically, even as butterflies' small colonies are difficult to protect, small, dispersed colonies also make it likely that most butterflies will escape total destruction. But the decline of butterfly numbers as a whole indicates the extent to which our environment has been robbed of its natural features. And unless people are educated about butterflies' needs and dangers, the fate of the Xerces Blue awaits many more species. Butterfly gardeners may have the satisfaction of playing a small role in preserving our rich butterfly resource.

# APPENDICES

# APPENDICES

## FIFTY COMMON GARDEN BUTTERFLIES

The following list contains fifty common species of butterflies that you may be able to attract to your garden. While not all of these occur regularly in towns and gardens, each should be compatible to butterfly garden culture. Representatives have been selected from each region of the country. The ranges refer to distribution in the lower forty-eight states.

### BRUSH-FOOTED BUTTERFLIES (Nymphalidae)

**American Painted Lady**
*(Vanessa virginiensis)*

RANGE: Entire U. S., but much scarcer in the West than in the East.
FOOD PLANT: Various species of everlasting, including pearly everlasting (*Anaphalis margaritacea*), sweet everlasting (*Gnaphalium obtusifolium*), plantain-leaved pussy toes (*Antennaria plantaginifolia*); other members of the daisy family (Compositae), including burdock (*Arctium*), ironweed (*Vernonia*), wormwood (*Artemisia*).
NECTAR PREFERENCES: Composites such as thistle, knapweed, common yarrow, goldenrod, aster, marigold, and zinnia;

also milkweed, butterfly bush, mallow, buttonbush, red clover, vetch, mint, self-heal, privet, scabiosa, dogbane, sweet pepperbush, winter cress, salt heliotrope.
ON WING: May-November, year-round in far South.
BROODS: Two–four.
HIBERNATES AS: Adult or chrysalis.
HABITATS: Open areas, meadows, streamsides.
SPECIAL FEATURES: Adults may be able to overwinter in North. Exhibits some emigratory behavior. Butterfly often basks on bare ground. Visits moist spots. Eggs laid singly. Caterpillar constructs nest of silk, leaves, and other plant material. Large "eye spots" distinguish it from other ladies.

**Buckeye**
*(Junonia coenia)*

RANGE: Southern U.S., spreading northward in summer.
FOOD PLANT: Various members of the snapdragon family (Scrophulariaceae), including snapdragon (*Antirrhinum*), toadflax (*Linaria*), false foxglove (*Aureolaria*), monkey flower (*Mimulus*), figwort (*Scrophularia*); plantain (*Plantago*); verbena (*Verbena*); ruellia (*Ruellia nodiflora*).

NECTAR PREFERENCES: Composites such as aster, knapweed, gumweed, tickseed-sunflower, chicory, and coreopsis; also plantain, wild buckwheat, peppermint, dogbane, milkweed.

ON WING: March-October, year-round in far South.

BROODS: Two–four.

HIBERNATES AS: Probably unable to hibernate in cold areas.

HABITATS: Open areas, meadows, fields, roadsides, shorelines.

SPECIAL FEATURES: Emigrates northward in spring, broadly in fall. Fond of basking on bare ground and visiting mud puddles. Exhibits territorial behavior. Males perch and patrol, searching for females. Impermanent garden guests, except in the South.

**Comma**
*(Polygonia comma)*

RANGE: Entire U.S. from Great Plains east.

FOOD PLANT: Hops (*Humulus*), nettle (*Urtica*), false nettle (*Boehmeria cylindrica*), wood nettle (*Laportea canadensis*), elm (*Ulmus*).

NECTAR PREFERENCES: Rotting fruit, sap, flowers such as butterfly bush, ivy, Michaelmas daisy, hebe, showy stonecrop, dandelion.

ON WING: Spring-fall.

BROODS: Two in North, three in South.

HIBERNATES AS: Adult.

HABITATS: Open woodlands, streamsides, roadsides.

SPECIAL FEATURES: Silvery "comma" mark on underside of each hindwing. Butterfly also called the Hop Merchant, because of its caterpillars' fondness for hops. Caterpillar constructs a shelter from a leaf of the food plant. Habits similar to Question Mark; both have early and late season forms.

**Great Spangled Fritillary**
*(Speyeria cybele)*

RANGE: Most of U.S., except extreme Southeast.

FOOD PLANT: Various species of violet (*Viola*).

NECTAR PREFERENCES: Composites such as thistle, Joe-Pye-weed, ironweed, black-eyed Susan, and purple coneflower; also cardinal flower, bergamot, red clover, vetch, milkweed, verbena, mountain laurel, New Jersey tea.

ON WING: June-September.

BROODS: One.

HIBERNATES AS: Newly hatched caterpillar.

HABITATS: Open areas, woodlands, moist meadows, roadsides.

SPECIAL FEATURES: The largest fritillary. Especially fond of thistles. Floats with a slow, gradual flight when relaxed and pauses to nectar at length, affording excellent photographic opportunities.

**Gulf Fritillary**
*(Agraulis vanillae)*

RANGE: Southern U.S., visiting middle latitudes in summer.

FOOD PLANT: Various species of passion flower (*Passiflora*).

NECTAR PREFERENCES: Lantana, composites such as beggar-ticks and thistle; also passion flower, cordia.

ON WING: Early spring to winter, year-round in far South.

BROODS: Multiple.

HIBERNATES AS: Cannot overwinter where frost occurs.

HABITATS: Open areas, fields, forest edges, pastures, canyons.

SPECIAL FEATURES: Emigrates north. Fast-flying. Males patrol in search of females. A very suitable butterfly for southern cities, easy to rear and habituate to gardens. A longwing rather than a true fritillary, yet silver-spotted and spectacular.

**Hackberry Butterfly**
*(Asterocampa celtis)*

RANGE: Most of U.S. east of the Dakotas, and Arizona.

FOOD PLANT: Various species of hackberry (*Celtis*).

NECTAR PREFERENCES: Rotting fruit, sap, dung, carrion, flowers such as milkweed.

ON WING: May-October, depending on location.

BROODS: One or two in North, three in South.

HIBERNATES AS: Egg or caterpillar.

HABITATS: Woodlands, forest edges, watercourses, roadsides, parks, cemeteries, suburbs.

SPECIAL FEATURES: Often perches on hackberry trees or other posts such as signs, headstones, or persons standing still. Can become extremely numerous. Easily lured to overripe bananas, and reared from the attractive green caterpillars and chrysalises. Another hackberry feeder, the Tawny Emperor (A. clyton), may be more common in your area.

## Milbert's Tortoiseshell
(Aglais milberti)

RANGE: Northern U.S., occasionally in South.

FOOD PLANT: Nettle (Urtica).

NECTAR PREFERENCES: Rotting fruit, sap, composites such as thistle, sneezeweed, Gloriosa daisy, Shasta daisy, Michaelmas daisy, ox-eye daisy, goldenrod, aster, marigold, and ageratum; also butterfly bush, lilac, stonecrop, showy stonecrop, rock cress, Siberian wallflower.

ON WING: March-November.

BROODS: Two-three.

HIBERNATES AS: Adult.

HABITATS: Woodlands, forest edges, fields, meadows, riversides, roadsides.

SPECIAL FEATURES: Appears in early spring, often pale and tattered after hibernating in a hollow tree or outbuilding. May take wing on sunny days in midwinter. Fresh, colorful new individuals come out in early summer. One of the best all-round garden butterflies.

## Mourning Cloak
(Nymphalis antiopa)

RANGE: Entire U.S.

FOOD PLANT: Willow (Salix), elm (Ulmus), poplar, aspen, cottonwood (Populus), birch (Betula), hackberry (Celtis).

NECTAR PREFERENCES: Rotting fruit, sap, flowers such as butterfly bush, milkweed, moss pink, New Jersey tea, rock cress, dogbane, mountain andromeda, pussy willows, composites such as Shasta daisy.

ON WING: Year-round.

BROODS: One-three.

HIBERNATES AS: Adult.

HABITATS: Open woodlands, riversides, forest edges.

SPECIAL FEATURES: Possibly the longest-lived North American butterfly, it may survive for more than ten months. Often the first butterfly on wing in spring, as it comes out of hibernation. Eggs laid in clusters. Caterpillars feed communally in a silk web at first, singly during the last two instars. Perches on branches, stumps, and other features (even an outstretched hand) for pursuit of mate. A fine garden butterfly that may surprise you by flying in February.

## Painted Lady
(Vanessa cardui)

RANGE: Entire U.S., but ephemeral.

FOOD PLANT: Various members of the daisy family (Compositae), including thistle (Cirsium), knapweed (Centaurea), burdock (Arctium), groundsel (Senecio), sunflower (Helianthus), pearly everlasting (Anaphalis margaritacea), wormwood (Artemisia); members of the borage family (Boraginaceae); members of the mallow family (Malvaceae), including hollyhock (Althaea), common mallow (Malva neglecta).

NECTAR PREFERENCES: Composites such as thistle, dandelion, Joe-Pye-weed, ironweed, gayfeather, rabbitbrush, aster, Michaelmas daisy, zinnia, cosmos, and dahlia; also butterfly bush, buttonbush, bee balm, mint, sweet William, valerian, red clover, showy stonecrop, privet, candytuft, milkweed, Siberian wallflower, scabiosa, mallow.

ON WING: Spring-fall in North, year-round in far South.
BROODS: One-four.
HIBERNATES AS: Unable to overwinter in cold areas.
HABITATS: Open areas, meadows, mountains, deserts.
SPECIAL FEATURES: Mass emigrations repopulate North America from the South each year. Number of emigrants fluctuates from year to year, but occasionally reaches monumental proportions. Weak southward emigrations may occur in autumn. The "Cosmopolitan Butterfly" is a beloved garden visitor worldwide.

## Pearly Crescentspot
*(Phyciodes tharos)*

RANGE: Entire U.S. except Pacific Coast.
FOOD PLANT: Various species of aster (*Aster*).
NECTAR PREFERENCES: Composites such as aster, thistle, showy daisy, black-eyed Susan, hawkweed, fleabane, beggar-ticks, and tickseed-sunflower; also dogbane, white clover, sticky geranium, winter cress, milkweed, peppermint.
ON WING: April-November, year-round in far South.
BROODS: One-five, or more.
HIBERNATES AS: Half-grown caterpillar.
HABITATS: Open areas, fields, moist meadows, streamsides, roadsides.
SPECIAL FEATURES: Pugnacious or inquisitive butterfly, often darting after passing objects. Newly emerged males visit moist ground and streamsides and patrol their territories in the garden. Eggs laid in clusters, larvae feed communally.

## Question Mark
*(Polygonia interrogationis)*

RANGE: Entire U.S. east of Rockies.
FOOD PLANT: Nettle (*Urtica*), false nettle (*Boehmeria cylindrica*), hops (*Humulus*), elm (*Ulmus*), hackberry (*Celtis*).
NECTAR PREFERENCES: Rotting fruit, sap,

dung, carrion, flowers such as aster, milkweed, sweet pepperbush.
ON WING: Spring to fall.
BROODS: Two-five.
HIBERNATES AS: Adult.
HABITATS: Open woodlands, streamsides, orchards, roadsides.
SPECIAL FEATURES: Silvery "question mark" on underside of each hindwing, formed by a swirl and nearby dot. Butterfly emigrates widely in the fall, and sometimes overwinters in large groups. May become intoxicated by drinking the juices of fermented fruit. Males often land on tree trunks, visit mud, and exhibit territorial behavior. Females usually oviposit on a plant near the host, laying their eggs in columns, horizontal strings, or singly.

## Red Admiral
*(Vanessa atalanta)*

RANGE: Entire U.S. during summer and fall.
FOOD PLANT: Various members of the nettle family (Urticaceae), including stinging nettle (*Urtica dioica*), tall wild nettle (*U. gracilis*), false nettle (*Boehmeria cylindrica*), wood nettle (*Laportea canadensis*), pellitory (*Parietaria*), hops (*Humulus*).
NECTAR PREFERENCES: Rotting fruit, sap, composites such as Michaelmas daisy, aster, thistle, dandelion, gumweed, daisy, goldenrod, beggar-ticks, Gloriosa daisy, Shasta daisy, gayfeather, dahlia, and ageratum; also butterfly bush, milkweed, candytuft, alfalfa, showy stonecrop, dogbane, Siberian wallflower, hebe, sweet pepperbush, ivy, fireweed, red clover, mallow, sea holly, mint, valerian.
ON WING: April-October, year-round in the far South.
BROODS: One-three.
HIBERNATES AS: Rarely as an adult; generally unable to overwinter in North.
HABITATS: Open woodlands, forest edges, meadows, streamsides, roadsides, yards, and parks.
SPECIAL FEATURES: Emigrates north each spring. Some individuals may emigrate south in autumn. Acts territorial, male

*110*

perches and darts out after females and other passing objects, often alights on people in gardens, and is generally well habituated to human environments. Caterpillars make nettle-leaf shelters and help keep nettles in check. A favorite of many gardeners.

### Red-spotted Purple
*(Basilarchia astyanax)*

RANGE: Entire U.S. east of Rockies; southern Arizona.
FOOD PLANT: Willow (*Salix*), aspen, poplar (*Populus*), cherry, plum (*Prunus*), oak (*Quercus*), hawthorn (*Crataegus*), apple (*Malus*), hornbeam (*Carpinus*), gooseberry (*Ribes*), deerberry (*Vaccinium stamineum*).
NECTAR PREFERENCES: Rotting fruit, sap, dung, carrion, aphid honeydew, flowers such as cardinal flower, viburnum, spiraea, privet, Hercules-club, sweet pepperbush.
ON WING: May-October, earlier in far South.
BROODS: Two-three.
HIBERNATES AS: Young caterpillar.
HABITATS: Open woodlands, forest edges, streamsides, meadows.
SPECIAL FEATURES: Mimics the Pipevine Swallowtail. In the northern part of range, hybridizes with the White Admiral, and many consider them to be the same species. Often basks on roads and sidewalks, displaying its brilliant metallic-blue wings.

### Satyr Anglewing
*(Polygonia satyrus)*

RANGE: Western U.S. from eastern edge of Rockies to the Pacific; occasionally in extreme north of eastern U.S.
FOOD PLANT: Nettle (*Urtica*).
NECTAR PREFERENCES: Rotting fruit, sap, flowers such as blackberry, almond.
ON WING: Early spring to late fall.
BROODS: Two or more.
HIBERNATES AS: Adult.
HABITATS: Open woodlands, streamsides, roadsides, parks, and glades.

SPECIAL FEATURES: Fond of dappled riverbanks. Camouflaged against tree bark, startles birds with bright upperside revealed in flight. Likes to bask in bright sun with wings spread open.

### Viceroy
*(Basilarchia archippus)*

RANGE: Most of U.S. from Atlantic west through Great Basin.
FOOD PLANT: Willow (*Salix*), aspen, poplar (*Populus*), apple (*Malus*), plum, cherry (*Prunus*).
NECTAR PREFERENCES: Rotting fruit, sap, dung, carrion, aphid honeydew, composites such as thistle, aster, Joe-Pye-weed, goldenrod, and beggar-ticks; also milkweed.
ON WING: April-September, almost year-round farther South.
BROODS: One or two in North, three or more in South.
HIBERNATES AS: Young caterpillar.
HABITATS: Open areas, streamsides, marshes, meadows, roadsides.
SPECIAL FEATURES: Palatable mimic of the distasteful Monarch. In the southern part of range, mimics the darker Queen. Behavior and biology similar to White Admiral and Red-spotted Purple, since they are all closely related admirals despite their different appearances.

### West Coast Lady
*(Vanessa annabella)*

RANGE: Western U.S. from Great Plains to Pacific Coast.
FOOD PLANT: Various members of the mallow family (Malvaceae), including cheeseweed (*Malva parviflora*), hollyhock (*Althaea*), globemallow (*Sphaeralcea*), sidalcea (*Sidalcea*); nettle (*Urtica*).
NECTAR PREFERENCES: Butterfly bush, cheeseweed, mallow, mint, statice, composites such as aster, thistle, marigold.
ON WING: Early spring to late fall, year-round in far South.

*111*

BROODS: Multiple.

HIBERNATES AS: May not be able to resist frost in any stage.

HABITATS: Open areas, fields, mountains.

SPECIAL FEATURES: Population fluctuates from year to year, but without the Painted Lady's mass movement. Some individuals emigrate, for example, into the Rockies from farther west. Butterfly fond of basking on bare ground and hilltops with other individuals.

## White Admiral
*(Basilarchia arthemis)*

RANGE: Northeastern U.S. from Minnesota to New England.

FOOD PLANT: Birch (*Betula*), aspen, poplar (*Populus*), willow (*Salix*), hawthorn (*Crataegus*), basswood (*Tilia*), American hornbeam (*Carpinus caroliniana*), shadbush (*Amelanchier*).

NECTAR PREFERENCES: Rotting fruit, sap, dung, carrion, aphid honeydew, various flowers.

ON WING: June-August.

BROODS: One-two.

HIBERNATES AS: Young caterpillar.

HABITATS: Open woodlands, forest edges, roadsides.

SPECIAL FEATURES: Often perches high above ground, then darts out after passing objects. Caterpillar overwinters in a hibernaculum constructed from a rolled-up leaf. These may be found and brought into the garden for emergence in spring.

## GOSSAMER WINGS
*(Lycaenidae)*

## Brown Elfin
*(Incisalia augustinus)*

RANGE: Most of U.S.

FOOD PLANT: Various members of the heath family (*Ericaceae*) in East, including blueberry (*Vaccinium*), azalea (*Rhododendron*), sugar huckleberry (*Vaccinium vacillans*), leatherleaf (*Chamaedaphne*), bearberry (*Arctostaphylos uva-ursi*), huckleberry (*Gaylussacia*), Labrador tea (*Ledum groenlandicum*); in West, dodder (*Cuscata*), California lilac (*Ceanothus*), salal (*Gaultheria*), apple (*Malus*), madrone (*Arbutus*).

NECTAR PREFERENCES: Winter cress, blueberry, bitter cherry, wild buckwheat, footsteps of spring, willow, bearberry, wild plum, bitterbrush.

ON WING: April-June.

BROODS: One.

HIBERNATES AS: Chrysalis.

HABITATS: Forest edges, open woodlands, acid bogs, pine barrens.

SPECIAL FEATURES: Spring butterfly, in general. Visits moist ground and streamsides. Males perch and dart out after females and other passing objects. Survives in urban settings where hosts abound.

## Common Blue
*(Icaricia icarioides)*

RANGE: Most of western U.S.

FOOD PLANT: Various species of lupine (*Lupinus*).

NECTAR PREFERENCES: Lupine, milkweed, various composites.

ON WING: April-August, the lower the altitude and farther south, the earlier.

BROODS: One.

HIBERNATES AS: Half-grown caterpillar.

HABITATS: Meadows, streamsides, mountains, roadsides.

SPECIAL FEATURES: Always found near lupines. Visits puddles and flowers. Larvae are tended by ants. Best suited to a large western garden little changed from native grasslands.

## Eastern Pygmy Blue
*(Brephidium isophthalma)*

RANGE: Eastern U.S. coast from South Carolina to Florida, Louisiana, and sometimes Texas.

FOOD PLANT: Glasswort (*Salicornia*), saltwort (*Batis*).

NECTAR PREFERENCES: Saltwort, lippia, palmetto.

ON WING: February-September, year-round in far South.

BROODS: Multiple.

HIBERNATES AS: Perhaps unable to over-winter in the North.

HABITATS: Saltwater areas, tidal flats.

SPECIAL FEATURES: Smallest eastern butterfly. Coastal species. Males patrol near food plant, searching for females.

## Gray Hairstreak
*(Strymon melinus)*

RANGE: Entire U.S.

FOOD PLANT: Various plants in many families; favorites are members of the pea (Leguminosae) and mallow (Malvaceae) families, including clover (*Trifolium*), mallow (*Malva*), vetch (*Vicia*), beans (*Phaseolus*), tick-trefoil (*Desmodium*), bush clover (*Lespedeza*), cotton (*Gossypium*), hibiscus (*Hibiscus*); also corn (*Zea mays*), mint (*Lamiacea*), oak (*Quercus*), strawberry (*Fragaria*), hawthorn (*Crataegus*), and hops (*Humulus*).

NECTAR PREFERENCES: Milkweed, white sweet clover, winter cress, cape plumbago, goldenrod, yellow bee plant, mint, dogbane, bitterbrush, Queen Anne's lace, tick-trefoil, sweet pea.

ON WING: April-October, earlier in the far South.

BROODS: Two-four.

HIBERNATES AS: Chrysalis.

HABITATS: Open areas, fields, roadsides, chaparral, open forests.

SPECIAL FEATURES: One of our most common and omnivorous species. Emigrates widely. Males exhibit territorial behavior, often perch on shrubs and small trees and dart out after potential females and interloping males.

## Marine Blue
*(Leptotes marina)*

RANGE: Most of western U.S.

FOOD PLANT: Various members of the pea family (Leguminosae), including alfalfa (*Medicago sativa*), false indigo (*Amor-*

*pha*), beans (*Phaseolus*), sweet pea (*Lathyrus odoratus*), locoweed (*Astragalus*); also leadwort (*Plumbago*), wisteria (*Wisteria*).

NECTAR PREFERENCES: Cape plumbago, wild buckwheat, oleander, Mexican fire plant, salt heliotrope, *Haplopappus*.

ON WING: Year-round in South, emigrates north in summer.

BROODS: Multiple.

HIBERNATES AS: Overwinters in any stage in frost-free zones.

HABITATS: Open areas, streamsides, plains, foothills.

SPECIAL FEATURES: Emigrates northward in summer, dies off in the fall. Visits moist spots and follows watercourses in its wanderings.

## Silvery Blue
*(Glaucopsyche lygdamus)*

RANGE: Most of U.S.

FOOD PLANT: Various members of the pea family (Leguminosae), including wild pea (*Lathyrus*), vetch (*Vicia*), lupine (*Lupinus*), white sweet clover (*Melilotus alba*), deer weed (*Lotus scoparius*), locoweed (*Atragalus*).

NECTAR PREFERENCES: Coneflower and other composites, lomatium, bitter cherry, lupine.

ON WING: March-July, depending on latitude and altitude.

BROODS: One.

HIBERNATES AS: Chrysalis.

HABITATS: Open forests, fields, streamsides, prairies, mountain meadows, roadside seeps.

SPECIAL FEATURES: Spring butterfly that can be induced into the garden. Visits puddles and patrols near food plant. Larvae are tended by ants, which provide protection in return for honeydew.

## Spring Azure
*(Celastrina ladon)*

RANGE: Entire U.S.

FOOD PLANT: Dogwood (*Cornus*), ceanothus (*Ceanothus*), viburnum (*Viburnum*), cherry (*Prunus*), sumac (*Rhus*), meadowsweet (*Spiraea salicifolia*), blueberry (*Vaccinium*), black snakeroot (*Cimicifuga racemosa*), wingstem (*Actinomeris alternifolia*).

NECTAR PREFERENCES: Holly, privet, ceanothus, ivy, rock cress, winter cress, escallonia, blackberry, cotoneaster, milkweed, forget-me-not, dogbane, willow, spicebush, coltsfoot, dandelion, violet, cherry.

ON WING: January-October, depending on latitude.

BROODS: Usually one in North, two or three farther south.

HIBERNATES AS: Chrysalis.

HABITATS: Open woodlands, fields, roadsides, freshwater marshes, forest edges, townscapes.

SPECIAL FEATURES: Spring butterfly, in general. Males visit damp spots and droppings, and patrol and sometimes perch and dart out after females. A very good garden habitué.

## Western Pygmy Blue
(*Brephidium exilis*)

RANGE: Most of western U.S.

FOOD PLANT: Various members of the goosefoot family (Chenopodiaceae), including pigweed (*Chenopodium*), saltbush (*Atriplex*), pickleweed (*Salicornia ambigua*).

NECTAR PREFERENCES: Mexican fire plant, pigweed, salt heliotrope.

ON WING: Spring–fall, year-round in far South.

BROODS: Multiple.

HIBERNATES AS: May emigrate into cold areas in spring.

HABITATS: Disturbed areas, alkaline places, marshes.

SPECIAL FEATURES: Smallest western butterfly. Emigrates widely, so unpredictable in gardens. Larvae are tended by ants.

## MILKWEED BUTTERFLIES
(*Danaidae*)

### Monarch
(*Danaus plexippus*)

RANGE: Entire U.S. except extreme Northwest.

FOOD PLANT: Various species of milkweed (*Asclepias*); reported on dogbane (*Apocynum*).

NECTAR PREFERENCES: Milkweed, butterfly bush, composites such as goldenrod, beggar-ticks, tickseed-sunflower, Joe-Pye-weed, thistle, ironweed, gayfeather, Mexican sunflower, and cosmos; also dogbane, teasel, glossy abelia, lilac, buttonbush, lantana, mallow, various mints.

ON WING: Spring to fall over most of range, fall to spring in overwintering areas.

BROODS: Two-four in North, four-six or more in South.

HIBERNATES AS: None. Adult migrates to Mexico or California to overwinter in a few small sites.

HABITATS: Open areas, meadows, fields, roadsides, marshes.

SPECIAL FEATURES: Only butterfly to migrate north and south each year. Often roosts in large groups during migration. Overwinters in large congregations on trees. Distasteful to predators due to toxic milkweed hosts; mimicked by the palatable Viceroy. Our best-known and most beloved garden insect, virtually our national butterfly.

### Queen
(*Danaus gilippus*)

RANGE: Entire southern U.S.; occasionally strays northward.

FOOD PLANT: Various species of milkweed (*Asclepias*).

NECTAR PREFERENCES: Milkweed, fogfruit, (*Lippia lanceolata*), beggar-ticks, various daisies.

ON WING: April-November, year-round in far South.

*114*

BROODS: Multiple.

HIBERNATES AS: None, cannot overwinter in the North.

HABITATS: Open areas, meadows, fields, roadsides, prairies, deserts, waterways.

SPECIAL FEATURES: Distasteful to predators. Mimicked by the darker form of the Viceroy. Some individuals emigrate northward. Southern butterfly gardeners find this a very special resource. Males visit madder vine.

## SATYRS OR BROWNS
*(Satyridae)*

### Large Wood Nymph
*(Cercyonis pegala)*

RANGE: Most of U.S., except southern Florida, northern Maine, and northwest coast.

FOOD PLANT: Various species of grasses (Poaceae).

NECTAR PREFERENCES: Rotting fruit, sap, flowers such as alfalfa, purple coneflower, mint, spiraea, sunflower, fleabane, penstemon, virgin's-bower, ironweed.

ON WING: June-September.

BROODS: One.

HIBERNATES AS: Newly hatched caterpillar.

HABITATS: Woodsides, meadows, grasslands, marshes, roadsides.

SPECIAL FEATURES: Often lands on tree trunks. Males patrol glades, searching for females. Like other satyrs, flight is not strong but expert as the butterfly flits among grassblades. An unmowed grassy meadow is essential if you want wood nymphs around your garden.

## SKIPPERS
*(Hesperiidae)*

### Common Checkered Skipper
*(Pyrgus communis)*

RANGE: Entire U.S. except northern New England and coastal Northwest.

FOOD PLANT: Various members of the mallow family (Malvaceae), including mallow (*Malva*), cheeseweed (*Malva parviflora*), hollyhock (*Althaea*), hibiscus (*Hibiscus*), Sida, Sidalcea, velvet-leaf (*Abutilon*), globe mallow (*Sphaeralcea*), poppy mallow (*Callirhoe*).

NECTAR PREFERENCES: Composites such as aster, knapweed, red clover, fleabane, mistflower, and beggar-ticks; red clover.

ON WING: March-October, year-round in far South.

BROODS: Three or more.

HIBERNATES AS: Chrysalis or full-grown caterpillar.

HABITATS: Open woodlands, meadows, prairies, roadsides, riversides, vacant lots.

SPECIAL FEATURES: Emigrates widely, but also forms small colonies readily. Scarcely a vacant lot in its range lacks a Checkered Skipper patrolling back and forth. Its grayish colors and whirring flight make it appear bluish on the wing.

### Fiery Skipper
*(Hylephila phyleus)*

RANGE: Eastern and southwestern U.S.

FOOD PLANT: Various species of grasses (Poaceae), including Bermuda grass (*Cynodon dactylon*), St. Augustine grass (*Stenotaphrum secundatum*), bent grass (*Agrostis*), crabgrass (*Digitaria*), sugar cane (*Saccharum officinarum*).

NECTAR PREFERENCES: Lantana, aster, milkweed, thistle, glossy abelia, sweet pepperbush, statice, cape plumbago, sneezeweed, beggar-ticks, Felicia daisy, ironweed, bristly ox tongue, knapweed.

ON WING: Year-round in far South, shorter period farther north.

BROODS: Two-five.

HIBERNATES AS: Unable to overwinter in North.

HABITATS: Lawns, grasslands, fields, forest edges, roadsides.

SPECIAL FEATURES: Emigrates northward in spring. Audible when fluttering wings.

Males perch and dart out after females and other passing objects. Caterpillars construct shelters at base of grass and thereby escape damage from lawn mowers. A delightful and bright city skipper throughout its regular range.

### Silver-spotted Skipper
*(Epargyreus clarus)*

RANGE: Entire U.S., but sporadic.

FOOD PLANT: Various members of the pea family (Leguminosae), including locust (*Robinia, Gleditsia*), wisteria (*Wisteria*), tick-trefoil (*Desmodium*), hog peanut (*Amphicarpa bracteata*), beans (*Phaseolus*), kudzu (*Peuraria thunbergii*), acacia (*Acacia*), licorice (*Glycyrrhiza*).

NECTAR PREFERENCES: Honeysuckle, thistle, Joe-Pye-weed, gayfeather, zinnia, milkweed, iris, buttonbush, dogbane, viper's bugloss, everlasting pea, privet, winter cress, red clover, purple vetch, selfheal.

ON WING: May-September, year-round in far South.

BROODS: One in far North, two-four in South.

HIBERNATES AS: Caterpillar, in leaf tent.

HABITATS: Open woodlands, hillsides, roadsides, suburbs.

SPECIAL FEATURES: Exhibits territorial and seemingly pugnacious behavior, as males perch and occasionally patrol, searching for females. Audible when fluttering wings. Caterpillars construct shelters from leaves of the food plant and overwinter in them, then pupate in a loose cocoon among debris on the ground. A big, flashy skipper as happy in gardens as in wild habitats.

### Tawny-edged Skipper
*(Polites themistocles)*

RANGE: Entire U.S., except most of Northwest.

FOOD PLANT: Various species of grasses (Poaceae), including panic grass (Panicum), and bluegrass (*Poa*).

NECTAR PREFERENCES: Thistle, red clover, chicory, alfalfa, purple coneflower, *Houstonia*, dogbane.

ON WING: April-September, year-round in Florida.

BROODS: One-two or more.

HIBERNATES AS: Chrysalis.

HABITATS: Grasslands, open woodlands, moist meadows, fields, roadsides, lawns.

SPECIAL FEATURES: Prefers grasslands in East, open forest and boggy mountain lakesides in West. In the Midwest, it is the most common skipper of lawns. Not a pest, its ability to colonize lawn grass makes it an ideal garden butterfly.

## SWALLOWTAILS
*(Papilionidae)*

### Anise Swallowtail
*(Papilio zelicaon)*

RANGE: Most of western U.S.

FOOD PLANT: Various members of the carrot family (Umbelliferae), including fennel (*Foeniculum vulgare*), carrots, parsley, cow parsnip (*Heracleum maximum*), seaside angelica (*Angelica lucida*); citrus trees.

NECTAR PREFERENCES: Lomatium, penstemon, mint, zinnia, lantana, butterfly bush, coltsfoot.

ON WING: Spring to fall, year-round in South.

BROODS: One, two, or multiple broods.

HIBERNATES AS: Chrysalis.

HABITATS: Open areas, roadsides, mountains, deserts, shorelines.

SPECIAL FEATURES: Males congregate on hilltops and at mud puddles. Males also patrol, searching for females. Easy to rear.

### Eastern Black Swallowtail
*(Papilio polyxenes)*

RANGE: Eastern U.S. to Rocky Mountains; Arizona, New Mexico.

FOOD PLANT: Various members of the carrot family (Umbelliferae), including Queen Anne's lace (*Daucus carota*), cultivated carrot, celery, parsley, parsnip, dill, caraway; members of the citrus family (Rutaceae), including rue (*Ruta graveolens*), Texas turpentine broom (*Thamnosma texana*).

NECTAR PREFERENCES: Milkweed, thistle, phlox, clover, alfalfa, Queen Anne's lace, purple loosestrife.

ON WING: February-November, depending on latitude.

BROODS: Two in North, three in South.

HIBERNATES AS: Chrysalis.

HABITATS: Open fields, meadows, roadsides, streamsides.

SPECIAL FEATURES: Especially fond of vegetable gardens. Female mimics Pipevine Swallowtail. Newly emerged males visit damp areas. Males perch and patrol, searching for females.

## Giant Swallowtail
### (Heraclides cresphontes)

RANGE: Most of U.S., except extreme North.

FOOD PLANT: Various citrus trees (Rutaceae), including orange trees, common prickly-ash (*Zanthoxylum americanum*), Hercules-club (*Z. clava-herculis*), common hoptree (*Ptelea trifoliata*), rue (*Ruta graveolens*), sea amyris (*Amyris elemifera*).

NECTAR PREFERENCES: Lantana, Japanese honeysuckle, milkweed, lilac, goldenrod, orange blossom, azalea, dame's rocket, bougainvillea, bouncing bet.

ON WING: May-September in North, year-round in far South.

BROODS: Two in North, three in South.

HIBERNATES AS: Chrysalis.

HABITATS: Open woodlands, forest edges, roadsides, citrus groves, streamsides.

SPECIAL FEATURES: This species is the largest butterfly in North America. High flier, but often descends into gardens, especially ovipositing females. Caterpillar is called the "Orange Dog," and may become plentiful in citrus groves. Males often visit moist ground, and patrol areas, searching for females.

## Pipevine Swallowtail
### (Battus philenor)

RANGE: Most of U.S.

FOOD PLANT: Various species of pipevine, including Dutchman's pipe (*Aristolochia durior*), Virginia snakeroot (*A. serpentaria*), *A. californica* and *A. longiflora*.

NECTAR PREFERENCES: Thistle, lilac, honeysuckle, milkweed, butterfly bush, azalea, orchid, phlox, clover, bergamot, viper's bugloss, dame's rocket, teasel, petunia, fruit tree blossoms.

ON WING: January-November, depending on latitude.

BROODS: Two in North, three in South.

HIBERNATES AS: Chrysalis.

HABITATS: Open forests, fields, roadsides, meadows.

SPECIAL FEATURES: Distasteful to birds. Mimicked by the palatable female Eastern Black Swallowtail, female Ozark Swallowtail, dark female Tiger Swallowtail, Spicebush Swallowtail, Red-spotted Purple, and female Diana Fritillary. Males patrol areas, searching for females.

## Spicebush Swallowtail
### (Pterourus troilus)

RANGE: Most of U.S. east of Rockies.

FOOD PLANT: Spicebush (*Lindera benzoin*), sassafras (*Sassafras albidum*), tulip tree (*Liriodendron tulipifera*), sweet bay (*Magnolia virginiana*), common prickly ash (*Zanthoxylum americanum*), bay (*Persea*).

NECTAR PREFERENCES: Honeysuckle, thistle, jewelweed, milkweed, clover, Joe-Pye-weed, lantana, azalea, dogbane, sweet pepperbush, mimosa.

ON WING: Mid-April to mid-October, depending on latitude.

BROODS: Two in North, three in South.

HIBERNATES AS: Chrysalis.

HABITATS: Woodlands, fields, meadows, streamsides, pine barrens.

SPECIAL FEATURES: Mimics the Pipevine Swallowtail. Newly emerged males visit mud puddles and streamsides, patrol open areas.

*117*

## Tiger Swallowtail
*(Pterourus glaucus)*

RANGE: Entire U.S. east of Rockies.

FOOD PLANT: Cherry (*Prunus*), ash (*Fraxinus*), birch (*Betula*), aspen, cottonwood (*Populus*), tulip tree (*Liriodendron tulipifera*), willow (*Salix*), sweet bay (*Magnolia virginiana*), hop tree (*Ptelea trifoliata*), spicebush (*Lindera benzoin*), lilac (*Syringa vulgaris*), American hornbeam (*Carpinus caroliniana*).

NECTAR PREFERENCES: Butterfly bush, thistle, milkweed, Japanese honeysuckle, phlox, Joe-Pye-weed, clover, lilac, abelia, buttonbush, bee balm, ironweed, sunflower, dandelion.

ON WING: February-November, depending on latitude.

BROODS: One-three.

HIBERNATES AS: Chrysalis.

HABITATS: Woodlands, streamsides, roadsides, orchards, savannahs, towns.

SPECIAL FEATURES: Dark female form mimics Pipevine Swallowtail. High flier, but often descends into gardens, especially ovipositing females. Adults sometimes nectar in groups. Newly emerged males visit mud puddles and streamsides, and patrol, searching for females.

## Western Black Swallowtail
*(Papilio bairdii)*

RANGE: Montana, western U.S.

FOOD PLANT: Dragon wormwood (*Artemisia dracunculus*).

NECTAR PREFERENCES: Penstemon, mint, *Senecio*.

ON WING: May-September.

BROODS: Two.

HIBERNATES AS: Chrysalis.

HABITATS: Mountains.

SPECIAL FEATURES: Good for gardeners at higher elevations. The Northwest variety (*P.b. oregonius*), often considered a separate species, is the official Oregon State Butterfly.

## Western Tiger Swallowtail
*(Pterourus rutulus)*

RANGE: Most of western U.S.

FOOD PLANT: Alder (*Alnus*), aspen, poplar (*Populus*), willow (*Salix*), sycamore (*Platanus*).

NECTAR PREFERENCES: Butterfly bush, thistle, milkweed, lilac, phlox, teasel, glossy abelia, mint, blackberry, lilies, agapanthus (lily-of-the-Nile), hibiscus, lantana.

ON WING: February-July, depending on latitude.

BROODS: One-three.

HIBERNATES AS: Chrysalis.

HABITATS: Streamsides, roadsides, canyons, parks, townscapes.

SPECIAL FEATURES: Possibly the most visible western butterfly. Males visit mud puddles and streamsides, and establish territories. Caterpillar, with its big eyespots, resembles a green snake.

# WHITES AND SULPHURS
*(Pieridae)*

## Cabbage White
*(Artogeia rapae)*

RANGE: Entire U.S.

FOOD PLANT: Various members of the mustard family (Cruciferae), including cabbage, collards, broccoli, nasturtium (*Tropaeolum*), winter cress (*Barbarea*), mustard (*Brassica*), peppergrass (*Lepidium*); members of the caper family (Capparidaceae).

NECTAR PREFERENCES: Mustard, winter cress, arabis, aubrieta, dandelion, red clover, dogbane, aster, mint, selfheal, wild bergamot, hedge-nettle, milkweed, wild oregano, cinquefoil, bristly ox tongue, lantana.

ON WING: Early spring to late fall in North, year-round in far South.

BROODS: Three in North, seven or eight in South.

HIBERNATES AS: Chrysalis.

HABITATS: Open woodlands, forest edges, agricultural fields, plains, urban waste places.

SPECIAL FEATURES: Probably the most widespread butterfly in North America. Especially fond of vegetable gardens. Newly emerged males visit moist ground and streamsides. Not a native; introduced to Canada in the 19th Century. Sometimes pestiferous, but often valuable as the only butterfly around.

## California Dogface
*(Zerene eurydice)*

RANGE: California, W. Arizona.

FOOD PLANT: False indigo (*Amerpha*), clover (*Trifolium*), indigo bush (*Dalea*).

NECTAR PREFERENCES: Thistle, blue dicks, and its own hostplants.

ON WING: Spring to fall.

BROODS: Two.

HIBERNATES AS: Chrysalis.

HABITATS: Mountains, forest clearings, foothills.

SPECIAL FEATURES: "Dog's face" pattern adorns upperside of each forewing. Designated as California's official state insect. Males exhibit brilliant purplish sheen, lacking in the Dogface Butterfly.

## Checkered White
*(Pontia protodice)*

RANGE: Most of U.S., absent from Northwest.

FOOD PLANT: Various members of the mustard family (Cruciferae), including wild peppergrass (*Lepidium*), shepherd's purse (*Capsella bursa-pastoris*), winter cress (*Barbarea vulgaris*); bee plant (*Cleome*).

NECTAR PREFERENCES: Hedge mustard, winter cress, milkweed, aster, centaury, spreading dogbane, salt heliotrope.

ON WING: March-November, depending on latitude; year-round in some areas of California.

BROODS: Three in North, four in South.

HIBERNATES AS: Chrysalis.

HABITATS: Open areas, agricultural fields, roadsides, sandy places.

SPECIAL FEATURES: Males patrol in search of females. A good butterfly for altered landscapes and urban vacant lots; can be extremely abundant.

## Cloudless Giant Sulphur
*(Phoebis sennae)*

RANGE: Most of southern and eastern U.S., except extreme North.

FOOD PLANT: Senna (*Cassia*), partridge pea (*Chamaecrista cinerea*), clover (*Trifolium*).

NECTAR PREFERENCES: Lantana, geranium, hibiscus, cardinal flower, bougainvillea, morning glory, daisy, cordia, thistle.

ON WING: June-September, year-round in far South.

BROODS: Two in North, three in South.

HIBERNATES AS: Cannot overwinter in cold climates.

HABITATS: Open areas, roadsides, fields, beaches, streamsides.

SPECIAL FEATURES: Large numbers emigrate outward from dense populations, especially in autumn. Sometimes individuals roost communally. It wanders widely, leading this spectacular, clear yellow species to be seen far out of its normal breeding range. Caterpillar constructs nest from silk and leaves of host plant, and hides in it during the day.

## Common Sulphur
*(Colias philodice)*

RANGE: Entire U.S., except most of Florida.

FOOD PLANT: Various members of the pea family (Leguminosae), including white clover (*Trifolium repens*), other clovers (*Trifolium*), trefoil (*Lotus*), vetch (*Vicia*), alfalfa (*Medicago*), white sweet clover (*Melilotus alba*).

NECTAR PREFERENCES: Clover, goldenrod, dandelion, aster, tickseed-sunflower, knapweed, milkweed, phlox, dogbane, winter cress.

ON WING: March-December, according to location.

BROODS: Three-five, depending on latitude.

HIBERNATES AS: Chrysalis.

HABITATS: Open areas, agricultural fields, roadsides, meadows.

SPECIAL FEATURES: Known as the Mud Puddle Butterfly, because large groups of males congregate at mud puddles. Especially fond of vegetable gardens and lawns. Very easy to rear.

### Dogface Butterfly
(*Zerene cesonia*)

RANGE: Most of southern U.S., Midwest; occasionally Northeast.

FOOD PLANT: Various members of the pea family (Leguminosae), including false indigo (*Amphora*), clover (*Trifolium*), indigo bush (*Dalea*), prairie clover (*Pentalostemon*), soybean (*Glycine*).

NECTAR PREFERENCES: Alfalfa, coreopsis, *Houstonia*, verbena.

ON WING: Mid to late-summer in North, almost year-round in South.

BROODS: Three.

HIBERNATES AS: Chrysalis or adult.

HABITATS: Open woodlands, deserts, prairies.

SPECIAL FEATURES: Note "dog's face" on upperside of each forewing. Butterfly emigrates northward. Newly emerged males visit puddles and patrol for females.

### Falcate Orangetip
(*Anthocharis midea*)

RANGE: Eastern U.S. from Massachusetts to Wisconsin, south to Georgia, Louisiana, and central Texas.

FOOD PLANT: Various members of the mustard family (Cruciferae), including rock cress (*Arabis*), bitter cress (*Cardamine*), winter cress (*Barbarea*), hedge mustard (*Sisymbrium*), shepherd's purse (*Capsella*

bursa-pastoris*), cut-leaved toothwort (*Centaria laciniata*).

NECTAR PREFERENCES: Cresses, peppergrass, mustard, wild strawberry, violet, toothwort, chickweed, spring-beauty, wild plum.

ON WING: March-June.

BROODS: One in North, two in South.

HIBERNATES AS: Chrysalis.

HABITATS: Open woodlands, streamsides, pine barrens, roadsides.

SPECIAL FEATURES: Spring butterfly. Low-flying. Will fly on cloudy days. Males patrol areas, searching for females, and sometimes congregate on hilltops.

### Orange Sulphur
(*Colias eurytheme*)

RANGE: Entire U.S.

FOOD PLANT: Various members of the pea family (Leguminosae), including alfalfa (*Medicago sativa*), white clover (*Trifolium repens*), white sweet clover (*Melilotus alba*), vetch (*Vicia*), crown vetch (*Coronilla*), wild indigo (*Baptisia*).

NECTAR PREFERENCES: Alfalfa, clover, thistle, aster, goldenrod, coreopsis, tickseed-sunflower, rabbitbrush, dandelion, salt heliotrope, milkweed, winter cress, dogbane, osier dogwood.

ON WING: March-December, depending on latitude.

BROODS: Three-five.

HIBERNATES AS: Chrysalis.

HABITATS: Open areas, alfalfa fields.

SPECIAL FEATURES: Also called the Alfalfa Butterfly, because of its caterpillars' fondness for alfalfa. Adults often roost in small groups. Newly emerged males visit moist ground and streamsides. Can be enormously abundant in alfalfa fields and clover meadows.

### Sara Orangetip
(*Anthocharis sara*)

RANGE: Much of U.S. from Rockies west.

FOOD PLANT: Various members of the mustard family (Cruciferae), including rock

120

cress (*Arabis*), mustard (*Brassica*), winter cress (*Barbarea*), hedge mustard (*Sisymbrium officinale*).

NECTAR PREFERENCES: Dandelion, strawberry, bitter cherry, monkey flower, blue dicks.

ON WING: February-July, according to altitude and latitude.

BROODS: One or two.

HABITATS: Woodlands, mountains, deserts, meadows, streamsides, fields.

SPECIAL FEATURES: Most abundant in spring. Low-flying and an avid nectarer, thus highly observable. Brilliant on the wing. Orange wingtips and green marbling on underside are very striking.

**Sleepy Orange**
*(Eurema nicippe)*

RANGE: Southern and southwestern U.S., most of eastern U.S. except extreme North.

FOOD PLANT: Various members of the pea family (Leguminosae), including senna (*Cassia*), clover (*Trifolium*).

NECTAR PREFERENCES: Beggar-ticks, other composites.

ON WING: March-November, depending on latitude; year-round in far South.

BROODS: Two-five.

HIBERNATES AS: Cannot overwinter in cold climates.

HABITATS: Forest edges, fields, meadows, roadsides, streamsides.

SPECIAL FEATURES: Emigrates northward, filling in much of the country with summer generations that die off in autumn. Males puddle and patrol.

# NECTAR SOURCES

## Cultivated Flowers

(Bloom period refers to an average latitude in a temperate zone.)

abelia (*Abelia*) shrub; white, pink, purple; summer–early fall

ageratum (*Ageratum*) annual; blue, white, pink; summer–fall

alder buckthorn (*Rhamnus frangula*) shrub or small tree; white; spring–summer

allium (*Allium*) bulb; pink, rose, violet, red, blue, yellow, white; late spring–summer

alyssum (*Alyssum*) perennial; yellow, white, pink; spring–fall

alyssum, sweet (*Lobularia maritima*) annual; white, pink, violet; spring–summer, longer in warmer areas

anemone (*Anemone*) perennial; blue, red, white, pink, rose, purple; early spring–fall

anthemis (*Anthemis*) perennial; yellow; summer–fall

arabis (*Arabis*) perennial; white, pink, purple; spring

aralia (*Aralia*) shrub-tree; white; mid-summer

aster (*Aster*) perennial; white, blue, red, purple; spring–fall

astilbe (*Astilbe*) perennial; white, pink, red; May–July

aubrieta, common (*Aubrieta deltoidea*) perennial; red, purple; early spring

barberry (*Berberis*) shrub; yellow, white; spring

beauty bush (*Kolkwitzia amabilis*) shrub; pink; May–June

bellflower (*Campanula*) perennial, biennial, annual; blue, purple, lavender, violet, white; spring–fall

blackberry; bramble (*Rubus*) shrub; white, pink; summer–fall

blackthorn (*Prunus spinosa*) shrub; white; spring

bleeding heart (*Dicentra*) perennial; pink, rose, white, yellow; spring–fall

blueberry; huckleberry (*Vaccinium*) shrub; white, pink; spring

buckeye (*Aesculus*) tree or large shrub; creamy; spring

*121*

buddleia (*Buddleia*) shrub or small tree; white, pink, violet; midsummer–fall

butterfly bush (*Buddleia davidii*) shrub or small tree; lilac with orange eye; midsummer–fall

butterfly weed (*Asclepias tuberosa*) perennial; orange; midsummer–early fall

buttonbush (*Cephalanthus occidentalis*) shrub or small tree; white; summer

calendula (*Calendula officinalis*) annual; orange, yellow; spring–midsummer; late fall through spring in milder areas

candytuft (*Iberis*) annual, perennial; white, pink, rose, purple, lavender, red; early spring–summer

caryopteris (*Caryopteris*) shrub; blue; late summer–fall

catmint (*Nepeta mussinii*) perennial; blue; early summer

catnip (*Nepeta cataria*) perennial; lavender, white; early summer

ceanothus (*Ceanothus*) shrub, small tree, ground cover; white, blue, pink; spring

cherry (*Prunus*) tree; white, pink; spring–fall

chestnut (*Castanea*) tree; white; summer

chives (*Allium schoenoprasum*) perennial; purple; spring

cinquefoil (*Potentilla*) perennial, shrub; yellow, white, pink; spring–fall

clematis (*Clematis*) vine, perennial; white, red, violet, pink, blue; spring–fall

coneflower, purple (*Echinacea purpurea*) perennial; purple; late summer

coreopsis (*Coreopsis*) annual, perennial; yellow, orange, red; late spring–fall

cornflower (*Centaurea cyanus*) annual; blue, pink, rose, red, white; summer

cosmos (*Cosmos*) annual; white, pink, rose, purple, yellow, lavender; summer–fall

cotoneaster (*Cotoneaster*) shrub; white, pink; spring

daffodil (*Narcissus*) bulb; yellow and white, with variations of orange, red, pink; spring

dahlia (*Dahlia*) perennial; many colors; summer–fall

daisy (*Chrysanthemum*) and other genera (see below)

daisy, gloriosa (*Rudbeckia hirta*) biennial or short-lived perennial, can be grown as an annual; yellow, orange, russet; summer–fall

daisy, Michaelmas (*Aster novi-belgii*) perennial; white, pink, rose, red, blue, violet, purple; late summer

daisy, Shasta (*Chrysanthemum maximum*) perennial; white, yellow; summer–fall

daisy bush (*Olearia haastii*) shrub; white; summer

daylily (*Hemerocallis*) perennial; orange, red, yellow, white; spring–fall

deutzia (*Deutzia*) shrub; white, pink; May–June

echium (*Echium*) biennial or shrubby perennial; blue, purple, rose, red; mid to late spring

English laurel (*Prunus laurocerasus*) shrub or small tree; white; summer

escallonia (*Escallonia*) shrub; red, white, pink; summer–fall, nearly year-round in mild climates

fleabane (*Erigeron*) perennial; white, pink, lavender, violet; early summer–fall

flowering tobacco (*Nicotiana*) perennial; white, red; summer

forget-me-not (*Myosotis*) annual, biennial, perennial; blue; early spring–fall

gaillardia (*Gaillardia*) perennial, annual; yellow, red, white, bronze; summer–fall

gayfeather (*Liatris*) perennial; purple; summer

gazania (*Gazania*) perennial; yellow, orange, white, pink; late spring and early summer, intermittently throughout the year in mild areas

geranium (*Pelargonium*) perennial; white, pink, red, purple, rose, lavender, violet, orange; summer, longer where protected

globe thistle (*Echinops exaltatus*) perennial; blue; midsummer–late fall

goldenrod (*Solidago*) perennial; yellow; summer–fall

gooseberry (*Ribes*) shrub; yellow, pink, red, purple; spring

hawkweed (*Hieracium*) biennial; yellow; midsummer

hawthorn (*Crataegus*) shrub or tree; white; spring

hazel (*Corylus avellana*) shrub; yellow; early spring

heath (*Erica*) shrub; white, red, pink, purple; year-round, depending on species.

heather (*Calluna*) shrub; pink, white, purple, lavender; summer–fall

hebe (*Hebe*) shrub; white, blue, purple, red; late spring–fall

heliotrope (*Heliotropium*) perennial; violet, white; spring–summer

honesty (*Lunaria annua*) biennial; purple, pink, white; late spring–early summer

honeysuckle (*Lonicera*) shrub or vine; orange, white, pink, red, purple, rose; early spring–fall

hyssop (*Hyssopus officinalis*) perennial; blue, white, pink, purple; midsummer–late fall

impatiens (*Impatiens*) annual, perennial; white, pink, rose, purple, red, orange, lavender; summer

ivy, English (*Hedera helix*) vine; greenish; late fall–winter

Jacob's ladder (*Polemonium caeruleum*) perennial; blue; spring–summer

Jupiter's beard (*Centranthus ruber*) perennial; red, white; late spring–early summer

lantana (*Lantana*) shrub; yellow, orange, red, purple, white, pink, lavender; year-round in frost-free areas

lavender (*Lavandula*) shrub; lavender, purple; almost year-round in mild areas

lilac (*Syringa*) shrub; purple, white, pink, lavender; spring

lily (*Lilium*) bulb; many colors; generally late summer

lily-of-the-Nile perennial; blue, white, purple; midsummer–early fall

linanthus (*Linanthus*) annual; lavender, white, pink, yellow; spring

lippia (*Phyla nodiflora*) perennial; purple, rose; spring–fall

lobelia (*Lobelia*) perennial, annual; red, blue, pink, purple, violet, white; early summer–late fall; winter in mild areas

lupine (*Lupinus*) annual, perennial, shrub; yellow, blue, white, pink, purple, red, orange; early spring–fall

marigold (*Tagetes*) annual; yellow, orange, maroon; early summer–late fall if old flowers are picked off

marjoram (*Origanum vulgare*) perennial; pink; midsummer

meadow saffron (*Colchicum autumnale*) corn; pink, purple, white; late summer

Mexican orange (*Choisya ternata*) shrub; white; early spring–summer

mignonette (*Reseda odorata*) annual; greenish-yellow; early spring–summer

mint (*Mentha*) perennial; purple; summer

mock orange (*Philadelphus*) shrub; white; late spring–early summer

monkshood (*Aconitum*) perennial; blue, purple; fall

nasturtium (*Tropaeolum*) perennial, generally grown as an annual; red, orange, yellow, white, bicolored; late summer

New Jersey tea (*Ceanothus americanus*) shrub; white; spring–summer

passion flower (*Passiflora*) vine; white, purple, pink, blue; summer

pear (*Pyrus communis*) tree; white; early spring

petunia (*Petunia*) tender perennial grown as an annual; pink, red, blue, purple, white; summer

phlox (*Phlox*) annual, perennial; white, purple, blue, pink, red, rose, lavender; spring–summer

pink (*Dianthus*) perennial, biennial, annual; pink, rose, red, yellow, orange; spring or summer, sometimes until frost

plum (*Prunus*) tree; white, pink; early spring

polyanthus (*Primula polyantha*) perennial; many colors; winter–spring

primrose (*Primula*) perennial; many colors; early spring–summer, sometimes longer

privet (*Ligustrum*) shrub or small tree; white; late spring–early summer

purple loosestrife (*Lythrum salicaria*) perennial; magenta, late summer

pussy willow (*Salix discolor*) shrub or small tree; pearl gray becoming yellow; late winter or early spring

redbud (*Cercis*) shrub or tree; pink, white, red, rose, purple; early spring

red-hot poker (*Kniphofia uvaria*) perennial; red, yellow, white; spring–summer

rockrose (*Cistus*) shrub; pink, white, purple; late spring–summer

rosemary (*Rosmarinus officinalis*) shrub; blue, purple; spring–fall

rose of Sharon (*Hibiscus syriacus*) shrub; white, red, blue, pink, purple; summer

sage (*Salvia*) annual, perennial, shrub; blue, purple, red, white, rose, lavender; late spring–late fall

scabiosa (*Scabiosa*) annual, perennial; purple, pink, blue, white, rose; June–late fall

sea holly (*Eryngium amethystinum*) perennial; blue, purple; midsummer–fall

senecio (*Senecio*) perennial, shrub, vine; yellow, red, white, pink, blue, purple; year-round in mild areas

showy stonecrop (*Sedum spectabile*) perennial; pink, rose, red; late summer–fall

snapdragon (*Antirrhinum*) perennial, usually treated as an annual; many colors; spring–summer

sneezeweed, common (*Helenium autumnale*) perennial; yellow, orange, red; summer–fall

spiraea (*Spiraea*) shrub; white, pink, red; spring–fall

spurge (*Euphorbia*) shrub, perennial, biennial, annual; yellow, orange, pink; late winter–spring

St. Johnswort (*Hypericum*) shrub, perennial; yellow; summer

statice (*Limonium*) annual, perennial; yellow, blue, purple, pink, white; spring–summer

stonecrop (*Sedum*) perennial; yellow, white, pink, red; spring–fall

sumac (*Rhus*) shrub or tree; white, pink, greenish; almost year-round in warm areas

sunflower (*Helianthus*) annual, perennial; yellow, orange, red-brown; late summer–fall

sunrose (*Helianthemum nummularium*) shrub; red, orange, yellow, pink, rose, white; spring–summer

sweet rocket (*Hesperis matronalis*) perennial; purple, white; spring–summer

sweet William (*Dianthus barbatus*) biennial often grown as an annual; white, pink, rose, red, purple, bicolored; spring–summer

thrift (*Armeria*) perennial; white, pink, rose, red; early spring–late fall

thyme (*Thymus*) perennial; pink, white, purple; June–September

tidytips (*Layia platyglossa*) annual; yellow; summer

toadflax (*Linaria*) annual, perennial; many colors, June–September

APPENDICES

valerian (*Valeriana officinalis*) perennial; white, pink, blue; mid–late summer

verbena (*Verbena*) perennial, some grown as annuals; white, pink, red, purple, blue; summer

viburnum (*Viburnum*) shrubs, rarely small trees; white, pink; early spring–summer

violet (*Viola*) perennial, some treated as annuals; white, blue, purple; spring–summer

viper's bugloss (*Echium vulgare*) annual; blue, purple, rose, white lavender; late summer

vitex (*Vitex*) shrub or tree; blue, white, pink; summer–fall

wallflower (*Cheiranthus cheiri*) perennial, biennial; yellow, orange, brown, red, pink, burgundy; spring–early summer

weigela (*Weigela*) shrub; red, white, pink, yellow; spring–fall

yarrow (*Achillea*) perennial; white, yellow, red; summer–early fall

zinnia (*Zinnia*) annual; many colors; summer–early fall

**Wildflowers**

(Close relatives of these examples may occur in regions other than those noted.)

alfalfa (*Medicago sativa*) blue, purple; May–October, year–round in some areas; widespread across U.S.

alpine sunflower (*Hymenoxys grandiflora*) yellow; July–October; western U.S.

aster (*Aster*) pink, purple, blue, white; June–November; widespread across U.S.

aster, New England (*Aster novae-angliae*) purple, rose; August–October; eastern U.S.

beggar-ticks; bur-marigold (*Bidens*) yellow; July–November; widespread across U.S.

bindweed, field (*Convolvulus arvensis*) white, pink; April–October; widespread across U.S.

blackberry; bramble (*Rubus*) white; May–July; widespread across U.S.

blackberry-lily (*Belamcanda chinensis*) orange; June–July; eastern U.S.

black-eyed Susan (*Rudbeckia hirta*) yellow; June–October; eastern U.S. and Rockies

blazing-star (*Liatris*) purple; July to frost; eastern U.S. and Rockies

bluebell (Campanulaceae) blue; May–August; widespread across U.S.

boneset (*Eupatorium perfoliatum*) white, purple; July–October; eastern U.S.

bouncing bet (*Saponaria officinalis*) pink, white; July–September; eastern U.S.

bugle (*Ajuga reptans*) blue; May–July; eastern U.S.

buttercup (*Ranunculus*) yellow; February–September; widespread across U.S.

butterfly weed (*Asclepias tuberosa*) orange, red; June–September; eastern U.S.

campion (*Silene*) white, pink; April–October; widespread across U.S.

campion, red (*Lychnis dioica*) red; June–September; northern part of eastern U.S.

cat's-ear (*Hypochoeris radicata*) yellow; March–August; northern part of eastern U.S., West

cinquefoil (*Potentilla*) yellow, purple, white, red; March–October; widespread across U.S.

clover, red (*Trifolium pratense*) red; April–October; widespread across U.S.

clover, white (*Trifolium repens*) white; May–October, year-round in some areas; widespread across U.S.

coltsfoot (*Tussilago farfara*) yellow; March-June; eastern U.S.

comfrey (*Symphytum officinale*) white, pink, purple, blue, yellow; June–September; eastern U.S.

coneflower (*Echinacea, Rudbeckia*) yellow; July–October; widespread across U.S.

cornflower (*Centaurea cyanus*) blue,

*125*

pink, white, purple; May–October; East, West

cuckoo-flower (*Cardamine pratensis*) white, pink; April–June; eastern U.S.

daisy, ox-eye (*Chrysanthemum leucanthemum*) white; May–October; East, West

dame's rocket (*Hesperis matronalis*) pink, purple, white; May–July; eastern U.S.

dandelion (*Taraxacum officinale*) yellow; early spring–late fall, year-round in some areas; widespread across U.S.

daylily (*Hemerocallis fulva*) orange; June–August; eastern U.S.

field scabious (*Knautia arvensis*) lavender; June–August; eastern U.S.

field sow–thistle (*Sonchus arvensis*) yellow; July–October; eastern U.S. and Rockies

figwort (*Scrophularia lanceolata*) green and brown; May–July; eastern U.S.

fireweed (*Epilobium angustifolium*) pink, purple; June–September; widespread across U.S.

flame azalea (*Rhododendron calendulaceum*) orange; May–June; eastern U.S.

fleabane, common (*Erigeron philadelphicus*) pink, purple, white; March–July; East, West

goatsbeard (*Tragopogon pratensis*) yellow; June–October; widespread across U.S.

golden Alexanders (*Zizia aurea*) yellow; April–June; eastern U.S.

goldenrod (*Solidago*) yellow; May–November; widespread across U.S.

groundsel, common (*Senecio vulgaris*) yellow; May–October, year-round in some areas; widespread across U.S.

harebell (*Campanula rotundifolia*) blue; June–September; widespread across U.S.

hawkweed (*Hieracium*) yellow, orange, white; May–October; widespread across U.S.

hawthorn (*Crataegus*) white, pink, red; May–June; widespread across U.S.

heather (*Calluna vulgaris*) pink; July–November; eastern U.S.

honeysuckle (*Lonicera*) yellow, white, orange; April–September; eastern U.S., Rockies, Northwest

hound's-tongue (*Cynoglossum officinale*) purple; May–August; widespread across U.S.

Indian hemp (*Apocynum cannabinum*) white, pink; June–September; East, West

ironweed (*Vernonia*) purple; July–October; eastern U.S.

Joe-Pye-weed (*Eupatorium*) purple; July–September; eastern U.S.

knapweed (*Centaurea*) pink, purple, white, rose; May–October; widespread across U.S.

lesser celandine (*Ranunculus ficaria*) yellow; April–June; eastern U.S.

lupine (*Lupinus*) blue, purple, pink, white, yellow; December–October; widespread across U.S.

mallow (*Malva*) pink, white, lavender; April–October, year-round in some areas; East, West

meadowsweet (*Spiraea latifolia*) pink, white; June–September; eastern U.S.

milkweed (*Asclepias*) many colors; April–August, March–December in some areas; widespread across U.S.

mustard (*Brassica*) yellow, white; January–October; East, West

phlox (*Phlox*) many colors; April–October; widespread across U.S.

primrose (*Primula*) pink, white, red, purple, blue; March–August; widespread across U.S.

purple loosestrife (*Lythrum salicaria*) purple; June–September; East, West

Queen Anne's lace (*Daucus carota*) white; May–October, year-round in some areas; East, West

ragged-robin (*Lychnis flos-cuculi*) pink, white; June–July; eastern U.S.
ragwort (*Senecio*) yellow; April–August; widespread across U.S.

sage (*Salvia*) blue, white, yellow, purple; March–July; East, West
selfheal (*Prunella vulgaris*) purple, blue; May–September; East, West
spearmint (*Mentha spicata*) purple, pink; June–October; widespread across U.S.
sunflower (*Helianthus*) yellow; June–October, February–November in some areas; widespread across U.S.
sweet-William catchfly (*Silene armeria*) pink; June–October; eastern U.S.

thistle (*Cirsium*) purple, white, yellow, rose, red; April–October; widespread across U.S.
toadflax (*Linaria vulgaris*) yellow; June–October; eastern U.S.

valerian (*Valeriana officinalis*) pink; June–July; eastern U.S.
verbena, vervain (*Verbena*) blue, purple, pink, white; June–September; East, West
violet (*Viola*) violet, white, blue, yellow; December–August; widespread across U.S.

water mint (*Mentha aquatica*) lavender; August–October; eastern U.S.
wild bergamot (*Monarda fistulosa*) purple; July–August; eastern U.S.
wild cherry (*Prunus*) white; April–May; widespread across U.S.
wild gooseberry (*Ribes*) yellow, white, pink; late April–early June; widespread across U.S.

wild lilac (*Ceanothus sanguineus*) blue; June–July; western U.S.
wild parsnip (*Pastinaca sativa*) yellow; May–October; eastern U.S.
woundwort (*Stachys palustris*) magenta; July–September; eastern U.S.

yarrow (*Achillea millefolium*) white, pink; March–November; widespread across U.S.
yellow bedstraw (*Galium verum*) yellow; June–August; northern part of eastern U.S.
yellow vetchling (*Lathyrus pratensis*) yellow; June–August; eastern U.S.

## WHERE TO GET PLANTS

*Nursery Sources: Native Plants and Wild Flowers.* Compiled by and available from the New England Wild Flower Society, Garden in the Woods, Hemenway Road, Framingham, MA 01701. Contains the names and addresses of 193 native plant nurseries in every state except Alaska and Hawaii. $2.50 each ($3.50 including postage and handling).

*Sources of Native Seeds and Plants.* Compiled by and available from the Soil Conservation Society of America, 7515 N.E. Ankeny Road, Ankeny, IA 50021. Contains the names and addresses of 272 growers and suppliers of native vegetation in forty states and Canada. $3.00 for single copies, postpaid ($2.50 each for ten or more copies, postpaid).

### Perennials and Wildflowers by Mail

Listed below are the members of the Mailorder Association of Nurserymen who catalog wildflowers and perennials. Catalogs may be ordered from any of these firms by writing to them directly at the addresses listed. Unless otherwise indicated, catalogs are free of charge; where there is a charge, it is usually deductible from the first order.

*127*

Vernon Barnes & Son
P.O. Box 250 LMN
McMinnville, TN 37110

Beersheba Wildflower Garden
P.O. Box 551
Stone Door, MN
Beersheba Springs, TN 37305
CATALOG PRICE: $1.00 Refundable

Bluestone Perennials
Dept. 47
7211 Middle Ridge Road
Madison, OH 44057

Burgess Plant & Seed Co.
905 Four Seasons Road
Bloomington, IL 61701

W. Atlee Burpee Seed Co.
Dept. MN, Burpee Building No. 12
Warminster, PA 18974

Clifford's Perennial & Vine
Rt. 2, Box 320 MN
East Troy, WI 53120
CATALOG PRICE: $1.00 (Deductible)

Daystar
RFD No. 2, Box 250 MN
Litchfield, ME 04350
CATALOG PRICE: $1.00

Dutch Gardens, Inc.
Dept. MN, P.O. Box 168
Montvale, NJ 07645

Dutch Mountain Nursery
7984 N. 48th Street, Dept M
Augusta, MI 49012
CATALOG PRICE: 50¢

Emlong Nurseries
2671M West Marquette Woods Road
Stevensville, MI 49127

Farmer Seed & Nursery Co.
Dept. M
Faribault, MN 55021

Henry Field Seed & Nursery Co.
Dept MN
407 Sycamore Street
Shenandoah, IA 51602

Fleming's Flower Fields
Dept. MAN, P.O. Box 4607
Lincoln, NE 68504

Gurney Seed & Nursery Corp.
110 Capitol Street
Yankton, SD 57078

H.G. Hastings Co.
P.O. Box 4274M
Atlanta, GA 30302

Holbrook Farm and Nursery
Route 2, Box 223B MN
Fletcher, NC 28732
CATALOG PRICE: $2.00

House of Wesley
2200M E. Oakland Avenue
Bloomington, IL 61701

Houston Daylily Gardens, Inc.
P.O. Box 7008, Dept. MN
The Woodlands, TX 77380
CATALOG PRICE: $2.00

Jackson & Perkins
Dept. MAN, P.O. Box 1028
Medford, OR 97501

J.W. Jung Seed Company
Dept. MN, Box 385
Randolph, WI 53956

Kelly Brothers Nurseries, Inc.
Dept. MN
Maple Street
Dansville, NY 11437

Krider Nurseries, Inc.
Dept. MAN, P.O. Box 29
Middlebury, IN 46540

Lakeland Nurseries Sales
Dept. MN, Unique Merchandise Mart
Building NR 4
Hanover, PA 17333

Lilypons Water Gardens
6865M Lilypons Road
Lilypons, MD 21717
CATALOG PRICE: $3.50

Earl May Seed & Nursery Co.
Dept. MN

208 North Elm Street
Shenandoah, IA 51603

Michigan Bulb Company
Dept MN
1950 Waldorf NW
Grand Rapids, MI 49550

McConnell Nurseries, Inc.
Dept. MAN
Port Burwell, Ontario, Canada NOJ ITO

George W. Park Seed Co.
Dept. MN, P.O. Box 32
Greenwood, SC 29640

Spring Hill Nurseries
Dept. MN
6523 North Galena Road
Peoria, IL 61601

Stark Bro's Nurseries
Box B2968A
Louisiana, MO 63353

Stern's Nurseries, Inc.
Dept. M
607 West Washington Street
Geneva, NY 14456

Sunnybrook Farms Nursery
P.O. Box 6 MN
9448 Mayfield Road
Chesterland, OH 44026
CATALOG PRICE: $1.00 (Deductible)

Swan Island Dahlias
P.O. Box 800 MN
Canby, OR 97013
CATALOG PRICE: $2.00 (Deductible)

Van Bourgondien Bros.
Dept. MN
245 Route 109
P.O. Box A
Babylon, NY 11702

Van Ness Water Gardens
2460M N. Euclid Avenue
Upland, CA 91786
CATALOG PRICE: $2.00

Vandenberg's
One Black Meadow Road

Chester, NY 10918
CATALOG PRICE: $1.00

The Wayside Gardens Co.
Dept. WG
Hodges, SC 29695
CATALOG PRICE: $1.00 (Deductible)

White Flower Farm
Dept. MN
Litchfield, CT 06759
CATALOG PRICE: $5.00

# WHERE TO GET BUTTERFLIES

Carolina Biological Supply Company, Burlington, NC 27215; or Powell Laboratories Division, Gladstone, OR 97027. Furnishes rearing kits with Painted Lady larvae for individuals and classes. Also offers moth rearing kits, and eggs, larvae, and cocoons of various moths.

Connecticut Valley Biological Supply Company, 82 Valley Road, P.O. Box 326, Southampton, MA 01073. Offers rearing kits with Painted Lady larvae for individuals and classes. Also offers moth rearing kits, and larvae and cocoons of various moths.

Insect Lore Products, P.O. Box 1535, Shafter, CA 93263. Offers "Butterfly Garden" rearing kits (including a classroom version) with larvae of the Painted Lady, Buckeye, or both. Also furnishes moth rearing kits.

John Staples, Breeder of Lepidoptera, 389 Rock Beach Road, Rochester, NY 14617. Offers eggs of the Eastern Black Swallowtail, Red Admiral, Orange Sulphur, and Common Sulphur; pupae of the Spicebush Swallowtail; and the eggs and pupae of various moths. Also offers a Moth Rearing Kit and a Special School Cocoon Collection.

Nasco, 901 Janesville Avenue, Fort Atkinson, WI 53538; or Nasco West, 1524 Princeton Avenue, Modesto, CA 95352. Offers rearing kits with Painted Lady larvae for individuals and classes. Also furnishes moth rearing kits and moth larvae.

"The Market Place" column in the *News of the Lepidopterists' Society* contains listings of butterfly eggs and pupae as well as moth eggs and cocoons available from individuals and companies. "Buy-Sell-Exchange-Wants" categories included. (See address under "Butterfly Organizations.")

"Trading Post" column in *Young Entomologists' Society Quarterly* includes livestock offered for sale and exchange. (See address under "Butterfly Organizations.")

Ward's Natural Science Establishment, 5100 West Henrietta Road, P.O. Box 92912, Rochester, NY 14692; or 11850 East Florence Avenue, Santa Fe Springs, CA 90670. Offers rearing kits with Painted Lady larvae for individuals and classes.

## WHERE TO GET ENTOMOLOGICAL EQUIPMENT

American Biological Supply Company
1330 Dillon Heights Avenue
Baltimore, MD 21228

BioQuip Products
P.O. Box 61
Santa Monica, CA 90406

Carolina Biological Supply Company
Burlington, NC 27215, or
Powell Laboratories Division
Gladstone, OR 97027

Connecticut Valley Biological Supply Company
82 Valley Road, P.O. Box 326
Southampton, MA 01073

Fisher Scientific Company
Educational Materials Division
4901 West LeMoyne Street
Chicago, IL 60651

Frey Scientific Company
905 Hickory Lane
Mansfield, OH 44905

Nasco
901 Janesville Avenue
Fort Atkinson, WI 53538; or
   Nasco West
1524 Princeton Avenue
Modesto, CA 95352

Ward's Natural Science Establishment
5100 West Henrietta Road
P.O. Box 92912
Rochester, NY 14692; or
11850 East Florence Avenue
Santa Fe Springs, CA 90670

## BUTTERFLY ORGANIZATIONS

Entomological Society of America
4603 Calvert Road
College Park, MD 20740
Publishes *The Bulletin of the Entomological Society of America, Annals, Journal of Economic Entomology,* and *Environmental Entomology.*

The Lepidoptera Research Foundation
c/o Santa Barbara Museum of Natural History
2559 Puesta Del Sol Road
Santa Barbara, CA 93105
Publishes *The Journal of Research on the Lepidoptera.*

The Lepidopterists' Society
SECRETARY, Julian P. Donahue
Natural History Museum of Los Angeles County
900 Exposition Boulevard
Los Angeles, CA 90007
Publishes the *News of the Lepidopterists'*

Society and the *Journal of the Lepidopterists' Society*.

The Xerces Society
The International Organization for Invertebrate Habitat Conservation
10 Southwest Ash St.
Portland, OR 97204
Publishes the newsletter *Wings* and the journal *Atala*.

Young Entomologists' Society
c/o Department of Entomology
Michigan State University
East Lansing, MI 48824
Publishes *Y.E.S. Quarterly*.

The Butterfly Club of America
736 Main Avenue
Suite 200, Box 2257
Durango, CO 81302
Plans to publish the newsletter *Chrysalis*.

In addition, there are several regional, state, and local organizations. Inquire at your local university or museum.

# WILDFLOWER, NATIVE PLANT, AND GARDENING ORGANIZATIONS

American Association of Botanical Gardens and Arboreta
P.O. Box 206
Swarthmore, PA 19081

American Association of Nurserymen
1250 I Street, N.W., Suite 500
Washington, D.C. 20005

American Horticultural Society
P.O. Box 0105
Mount Vernon, VA 22121

Mailorder Association of Nurserymen
210 Cartwright Boulevard
Massapequa Park, NY 11762

National Council of State Garden Clubs
4401 Magnolia Avenue
St. Louis, MO 63110

National Wildflower Research Center
2600 FM 973 North
Austin, TX 78725

The Garden Club of America
598 Madison Avenue
New York, NY 10022

"Botanical Clubs and Native Plant Societies—United States."
A list available for $1.00 from the New England Wild Flower Society, Garden in the Woods, Hemenway Road, Framingham, MA 01701. Contains listings for most states.

# FURTHER READING

The following list will give readers many sources of additional information on the subjects treated in the text.

**Butterflies**

Allen, James. "How to Photograph Butterflies." *Terra* 23/5 (1985):25–30.
Arnett, Dr. Ross H. Jr., and Jacques, Dr. Richard L., Jr. *Simon and Schuster's Guide to Insects*. New York: Simon and Schuster, 1981.
Bernard, Gary D. "Red-absorbing Visual Pigment of Butterflies." *Science* 203 (1979):1125–27.
Borror, Donald J., and White, Richard E. *A Field Guide to the Insects of America North of Mexico*. Boston: Houghton Mifflin, 1970.
Brewer, Jo. *Wings in the Meadow*. New York: Houghton Mifflin, 1967.
Brower, Lincoln P. "Ecological Chemistry." *Scientific American* 220/2 (1969):22–29.
Brower, Lincoln P. "Monarch Migration." *Natural History*, June/July, 1977.
Brown, F. Martin. *Colorado Butterflies*. Denver: Denver Museum of Natural History, 1957.
Christensen, James R. *A Field Guide to the Butterflies of the Pacific Northwest*. Mos-

cow, Idaho: The University Press of Idaho, 1981.

Comstock, John Adams. *Butterflies of California*. Los Angeles: published by the author, 1927.

Comstock, John Henry, and Comstock, Anna Botsford. *How to Know the Butterflies*. New York: D. Appleton and Company, 1904.

Dethier, V.G., and MacArthur, Robert H. "A Field's Capacity to Support a Butterfly Population." *Nature* 201 (1964):728–29.

Donahue, Julian P. "Strategies For Survival: the Cause of a Caterpillar." *Terra* 17/4 (1979):3–9.

Dornfeld, Ernst J. *The Butterflies of Oregon*. Beaverton, Oregon: Timber Press, 1980.

Dronamraju, K.R. "Selective Visits of Butterflies to Flowers: A Possible Factor in Sympatric Speciation." *Nature* 186 (1960):178.

Ebner, James A. *The Butterflies of Wisconsin*. Milwaukee Public Museum: Popular Science Handbook, 1970.

Ehrlich, Paul R., and Ehrlich, Anne H. *How to Know the Butterflies*. Dubuque, IA: Wm. C. Brown, 1961.

Ehrlich, Paul R., and Raven, Peter H. "Butterflies and Plants." *Scientific American* 216/6 (1967):104–13.

Eisner, T.; Silberglied, R.E.; Aneshansley, D.; Carrel, J.E.; and Howland, H.C. "Ultraviolet Video-Viewing: the Television Camera as an Insect Eye." *Science* 166 (1969):1172–74.

Emmel, Thomas C. *Butterflies: Their World, Their Life Cycle, Their Behavior*. New York: Alfred A. Knopf, 1975.

Emmel, Thomas C., and Emmel, John F. *The Butterflies of Southern California*. Los Angeles: Natural History Museum of Los Angeles County, 1973.

Ferguson, D.C. *Host Records for Lepidoptera Reared in Eastern North America*. Washington, D.C.: Agricultural Research Service, United States Department of Agriculture, Technical Bulletin No. 1521 (1975).

Ferris, Clifford D., and Brown, Martin F., eds. *Butterflies of the Rocky Mountain States*. Norman: University of Oklahoma Press, 1981.

Field, William D. *A Manual of the Butterflies and Skippers of Kansas*. Bulletin of the University of Kansas 39/10 (1938):3–328.

Ford, E.B. *Butterflies*. Revised edition. Glasgow: Collins, 1975.

Free, J.B.; Gennard, Dorothy; Stevenson, J.H.; and Williams, Ingrid H. "Beneficial Insects Present on a Motorway Verge." *Biological Conservation* 8 (1975):61–72.

Garth, John S., and Tilden, J.W. "Yosemite Butterflies: An Ecological Survey of the Butterflies of the Yosemite Sector of the Sierra Nevada, California." *The Journal of Research on the Lepidoptera* 2/1 (1963):1–96.

Gilbert, Lawrence E. "Ecological Consequences of a Coevolved Mutualism Between Butterflies and Plants." In *Coevolution of Animals and Plants*. Austin: University of Texas Press, 1975.

Gilbert, Lawrence E., and Singer, Michael C. "Butterfly Ecology." *Annual Review of Ecology and Systematics* 6 (1975):365–97.

Hamm, A.H. "Butterflies at Oxford." *The Entomologist's Monthly Magazine*, December, 1943: 279.

Hamm, A.H. "Butterflies and Silver-Y Moth (*Plusia gamma* L.) at Oxford." *The Entomologist's Monthly Magazine*, March, 1945: 58.

Hamm, A.H. "Butterfly and Other Visitors to Michaelmas Daisies." *The Entomologist's Monthly Magazine*, April, 1948: 91–93.

Hanson, F.E. "Comparative Studies on Induction of Food Choice Preferences in Lepidopterous Larvae." In *The Host-Plant in Relation to Insect Behavior and Reproduction*. New York: Plenum Press, 1976.

Harris, Lucien, Jr. *Butterflies of Georgia*. Norman: University of Oklahoma Press, 1972.

Headstrom, Richard. *Adventures with In-*

sects. New York: Dover Publications, 1982.

Hogue, Charles L. "Butterfly Wings: Living Pointillism." Los Angeles County Museum of Natural History Quarterly, 6/4 (1968):4–11.

Holland, W.J. The Butterfly Book. Garden City, NY: Doubleday, Doran & Company, 1931.

Howe, Robert W. "Wings Over the Prairie." Iowa Conservationist, September, 1984.

Howe, William H. Our Butterflies and Moths. North Kansas City, MO: True Color Publishing Company, 1963.

Howe, William H., ed. The Butterflies of North America. New York: Doubleday & Company, 1975.

Ilse, Dora. "New Observations on Responses to Colours in Egg-laying Butterflies." Nature 140 (1937):544–45.

Ilse, Dora, and Vaidya, Vidyadhar G. "Spontaneous Feeding Response to Colors in Papilio demoleus L." Proceedings of the Indian Academy of Sciences 43 (1956):23–31.

Kennedy, J.S. "Mechanisms of Host Plant Selection." In Readings in Entomology. Philadelphia: W.B. Saunders Company, 1972.

Klots, Alexander B. A Field Guide to the Butterflies of North America, East of the Great Plains. Boston: Houghton Mifflin, 1951.

Klots, Alexander B. "Flight of the Butterfly." USAir, June, 1983.

Klots, Alexander B., and Klots, Elsie B. 1001 Answers to Questions About Insects. New York: Grosset & Dunlap, 1961.

Langer, H., and Struwe, G. "Spectral Absorption by Screening Pigment Granules in the Compound Eye of Butterflies (Heliconius)." Journal of Comparative Physiology 79 (1972):203–12.

Lovell, John H. "Butterfly-Flowers." In The Flower and the Bee: Plant Life and Pollination. New York: Charles Scribner's Sons, 1918.

Masters, John H. "Collecting Ithomiidae With Heliotrope." Journal of the Lepidopterists' Society 22 (1968):108–10.

Miller, Lee D., and Brown, F. Martin. A Catalogue/Checklist of the Butterflies of America North of Mexico. The Lepidopterists' Society, Memoir No. 2, 1981.

Milne, Louis, and Margery. The Audubon Society Field Guide to North American Insects and Spiders. New York: Alfred A. Knopf, 1980.

Mitchell, Robert T., and Zim, Herbert S. Butterflies and Moths. New York: Golden Press, 1964.

Nabokov, Vladimir. "Butterflies." In Speak, Memory: An Autobiography Revisited. New York: G.P. Putnam's Sons, 1966.

Opler, Paul A. "Management of Prairie Habitats For Insect Conservation." Journal of the Natural Areas Association 1/4 (1981):3–6.

Opler, Paul A., and Krizek, George O. Butterflies East of the Great Plains. Baltimore: The John Hopkins University Press, 1984.

Ordish, George. The Year of the Butterfly. New York: Charles Scribner's Sons, 1975.

Orsak, Larry J. The Butterflies of Orange County, California. Irvine, CA: University of California, Irvine, Press, 1977.

Orsak, Larry J. "Buckwheat and the Bright Blue Copper." Garden, January/February, 1980.

Owen, Denis F. "Lessons From a Caterpillar Plague in London's Berkeley Square." Environmental Conservation, 2/3 (1975):171–77.

Parenti, Umberto. The World of Butterflies and Moths. New York: G. P. Putnam's Sons, 1978

Peterson, Roger Tory; Pyle, Robert Michael; and Hughes, Sarah Anne. A Field Guide to Butterflies Coloring Book. Boston: Houghton Mifflin, 1983.

Pyle, Robert Michael. Watching Washington Butterflies. Seattle: Seattle Audubon Society, 1974.

Pyle, Robert Michael. "Conservation of Lepidoptera in the United States." Biological Conservation 9 (1976):55–75.

Pyle, Robert Michael. "How to Conserve Insects for Fun and Necessity." *Terra* 17/4 (1979):18–22.

Pyle, Robert Michael. "Butterflies: Now You See Them . . ." *International Wildlife*, January/February, 1981.

Pyle, Robert Michael. *The Audubon Society Field Guide to North American Butterflies.* New York: Alfred A. Knopf, 1981.

Pyle, R.; Bentzien, M.; and Opler, P. "Insect Conservation." *Annual Review of Entomology* 26 (1981):233–58.

Schemske, Douglas W. "Pollinator Specificity in *Lantana camara* and *L. trifolia* (Verbenaceae)." *Biotropica* 8/4 (1976):260–264.

Scudder, Samuel Hubbard. *Frail Children of the Air: Excursions Into the World of Butterflies.* Boston: Houghton, Mifflin and Company, 1897.

Shaw, John. "Splendor in the Grass: Tips From a Professional on How to Photograph Insects." *Blair & Ketchum's Country Journal*, June, 1984.

Shepardson, Lucia. *The Butterfly Trees.* San Francisco: The James H. Barry Company, 1914.

Shields, Oakley. "Flower Visitation Records for Butterflies." *The Pan-Pacific Entomologist* 48 (1972):189–203.

Shields, Oakley; Emmel, John F.; and Breedlove, Dennis E. "Butterfly Larval Foodplant Records and a Procedure for Reporting Foodplants." *The Journal of Research on the Lepidoptera* 8/1 (1969–70):21–36.

Singer, Michael C., and Gilbert, Lawrence E. "Ecology of Butterflies in the Urbs and Suburbs." In *Perspectives in Urban Entomology.* New York: Academic Press, 1978.

Smart, Paul. *The Illustrated Encyclopedia of the Butterfly World.* New York: Chartwell Books, 1984.

Sonntag, Linda. *Butterflies.* New York: G.P. Putnam's Sons, 1980.

Struwe, Goran. "Spectral Sensitivity of the Compound Eye in Butterflies (*Heliconius*)." *Journal of Comparative Physiology* 79 (1972):191–96.

Swihart, C.A., and Swihart, S.L. "Colour Selection and Learned Feeding Preferences in the Butterfly, *Heliconius charitonius* Linn." *Animal Behavior* 18 (1970):60–64.

Swihart, Christine A. "Color Discrimination by the Butterfly, *Heliconius charitonius* Linn." *Animal Behaviour* 19 (1971):156–64.

Swihart, S.L. "The Neural Basis of Colour Vision in the Butterfly, *Heliconius erato.*" *Journal of Insect Physiology* 18 (1972):1015–25.

Teale, Edwin Way. *Grassroot Jungles: A Book of Insects.* New York: Dodd, Mead & Company, 1937.

Teale, Edwin Way. "The Journeying Butterflies." *Audubon*, September-October, 1954.

Tekulsky, Mathew. "Butterflies are Free: Where to Go Find Them." *Los Angeles Times You* magazine, September 27, 1977.

Tietz, Harrison M. *The Lepidoptera of Pennsylvania: A Manual.* State College, PA: The Pennsylvania State College School of Agriculture, Agricultural Experiment Station, 1952.

Tietz, Harrison M. *An Index to the Described Life Histories, Early Stages and Hosts of the Macrolepidoptera of the Continental United States and Canada.* Two volumes. Sarasota, Florida: Allyn Museum of Entomology, 1972.

Tilden, J.W. *Butterflies of the San Francisco Bay Region.* Berkeley: University of California Press, 1965.

Tyler, Hamilton A. *The Swallowtail Butterflies of North America.* Healdsburg, CA: Naturegraph Publishers, 1975.

Urguhart, F.A. *The Monarch Butterfly.* Toronto: University of Toronto Press, 1960.

Vane-Wright, Richard I, and Ackery, Phillip R., eds. *The Biology of Butterflies.* In Symposium of the Royal Entomological Society Series. London and Orlando, FL: Academic Press, 1984.

Watson, Allan, and Whalley, Paul E.S. *The Dictionary of Butterflies and Moths in Color*. New York: Simon and Schuster, 1983.

Weed, Clarence M. *Butterflies*. Garden City, NY: Doubleday, Doran & Company, 1926.

Wigglesworth, V.B. *The Life of Insects*. New York: The New American Library, 1968.

Williams, C.B. *The Migration of Butterflies*. Edinburgh and London: Oliver and Boyd, 1930.

Williams, Ted. "Butterflies are Full of Surprises." *National Wildlife*, August-September, 1979.

Zim, Herbert S., and Cottam, Clarence. *Insects*. New York: Golden Press, 1956.

**Butterfly Gardening**

Anderson, Ethel. "A Garden of Butterflies." *The Atlantic Monthly*, August, 1940.

Atwood, Edna Peck. "Violet Fancier." *Nature Magazine* 46/2 (1953):77–79.

Borkin, Susan Sullivan. "Plant a Butterfly Garden." *Lore* 34/2 (1984):7–11.

Brady, Philip. "Boarding House for Butterflies." *Nature Magazine* 51/4 (1958):188–90.

Brewer, Jo. "How to Attract Butterflies." *Horticulture*, July, 1969.

Brewer, Jo. "An Invitation to the Butterfly Meadow." *Defenders*, August, 1978.

Brewer, Jo. "Bringing Butterflies to the Garden." *Horticulture*, May, 1979.

Brewer, Jo. "Butterfly Gardening." *Xerces Society Self-Help Sheet No. 7*, 1982.

Buck, Margaret Waring. *In Yards and Gardens*. New York: Abingdon Press, 1952.

Cervoni, Cleti. "Butterfly Gardens." *Essex Life*, Spring, 1985.

Collman, Sharon J. "The Butterfly's World: Notes of a Butterfly Gardener." *University of Washington Arboretum Bulletin* 46/2 (1983):16–26.

Crane, Jocelyn. "Keeping House for Tropical Butterflies." *National Geographic*, August, 1957.

Cribb, Peter. "How to Encourage Butterflies to Live in Your Garden." *Insect Conservation News* (Amateur Entomologists' Society, U.K.) 6 (1982):4–10.

Crotch, W.J.B. "A Silkmoth Rearer's Handbook." *The Amateur Entomologist* 12 (1956):1–165.

Damrosch, Barbara. "A Butterfly Garden." In *Theme Gardens*. New York: Workman Publishing Company, 1982.

Dimock, Thomas E. "Culture Maintenance of *Vanessa atalanta rubria* (Nymphalidae)." *The Journal of Research on the Lepidoptera* 23 (1984):236–40.

Dimock, Thomas E. "Hidden Variation in *Agraulis vanillae incarnata* (Nymphalidae)." *The Journal of Research on the Lepidoptera*, in press.

Dirig, Robert. *Growing Moths*. Ithaca, NY: New York State College of Agriculture and Life Sciences, Cornell University, 4-H Members' Guide M-6-6, 1975.

Dirig, Robert. "Butterflies, Cabbages and Kids." *Teacher*, May/June, 1976.

Donahue, Julian P. "Take a Butterfly to Lunch: A Guide to Butterfly Gardening in Los Angeles." *Terra* 14/3 (1976):3–12 plus fold-out poster.

Donahue, Julian P. "How to Create a Butterfly Garden." First Day Cover Page. The Reader's Digest Association, Inc., 1977.

Druse, Ken. "Butterflies are Free, But You Can Lure Them to Your Garden With Their Favorite Flowers." *House Beautiful*, August, 1984.

*Dun's Business Month*. "Butterflies for Sale." May, 1984.

Ginna, Robert Emmett, Jr. "A Shared Passion for Bugs." *Yankee*, September, 1984.

Goodall, Nancy-Mary. "Flowers for Butterflies." *The Illustrated London News*, July, 1978.

Goodden, Robert. "Butterflies of the Garden and Hedgerow." Concertina Publications Limited. In the greeting-card series, "Cards to Keep," 1978.

Green, Timothy. "Beautiful Fliers Fill an

Indoor Jungle in Suburban London." *Smithsonian*, January, 1985.

Haas, Carolyn; Cole, Ann; and Naftzger, Barbara. *Backyard Vacation: Outdoor Fun in Your Own Neighborhood."* Boston: Little, Brown, and Company, 1980.

Harrison, George H. "A Farm Full of Butterflies." *Ranger Rick's Nature Magazine*, October, 1982.

Harrison, George H. "Boom Times for Backyard Habitat: How People Are Creating Havens for Wildlife in Their Own Backyards." *National Wildlife*, October-November, 1983.

Hastings, Boyd. "Where Dandelions Grow." *Organic Gardening*, April, 1981.

Headstrom, Richard. *Suburban Wildlife: An Introduction to the Common Animals of Your Back Yard and Local Park*. Englewood Cliffs, NJ: Prentice-Hall, 1984.

Heal, Henry George. "An Experiment in Conservation Education: The Drum Manor Butterfly Garden." *International Journal of Environmental Studies* 4 (1973):223–29.

Howe, William H. "What's in Your Backyard?" *The Lepidopterists' News* 12 (1958):130.

Hult, Ruby El. "Some Notes On My Butterfly Gardening and Butterfly Raising." *Wings* 4/3 (1978) and 5/1 (1978):11.

Jackson, Bernard S. *Butterflies of Oxen Pond Botanic Park*. St. John's, Newfoundland: Memorial University of Newfoundland, 1976.

Jackson, Bernard S. "How to Start a Butterfly Garden." *Nature Canada*, April/June, 1977.

Jackson, Bernard S. "Butterfly Farming in Newfoundland." *Canadian Geographic*, August/September, 1979.

Jackson, Bernard S. "Oxen Pond Botanic Park." *Garden*, November/December, 1981.

Jackson, Bernard S. "The Oxen Pond Botanic Park as a Reserve For Common Native Butterflies." *Atala* 7 (1981):15–22.

Jackson, Bernard S. "The Lowly Dandelion Deserves More Respect." *Canadian Geographic*, June/July, 1982.

Jackson, Bernard S. "The Botanical Garden's Role in Conserving Indigenous Butterflies." *Wings*, in press.

Joode, Ton de and Stolk, Anthonie. "The Butterfly and the Moth." *In The Backyard Bestiary*. New York: Alfred A. Knopf, 1982.

Kulman, H.M. "Butterfly Production Management." *University of Minnesota Agricultural Experiment Station Technical Bulletin* 310 (1977):39–47; revised version in press in *Atala*.

Lutz, Frank E. *A Lot of Insects: Entomology in a Suburban Garden*. New York: G.P. Putnam's Sons, 1941.

Malinsky, Iris. "The Pleasure of Flowers and Butterflies." *Los Angeles Times Home* magazine, December 11, 1977.

Measures, David G. "Butterflies In Your Garden." *Bright Wings of Summer*. Englewood Cliffs, NJ: Prentice-Hall, 1976.

Moran, B.K. "City Butterflies." *San Francisco*, April, 1982.

Morton, Ashley. "The Importance of Farming Butterflies." *New Scientist*, May 20, 1982.

National Wildlife Federation. "Attracting Butterflies to Your Backyard Wildlife Habitat." Leaflet available from NWF, 1412 Sixteenth Street, N.W., Washington, D.C. 20036.

National Wildlife Federation. *Gardening with Wildlife*. Washington, D.C.: NWF, 1974.

Neulieb, Robert and Marilyn. "With Care, You Can Coax Butterflies Into Residence." *The Christian Science Monitor*, June 27, 1982: 15.

Newman, L. Hugh. "When Churchill Brought Butterflies to Chartwell." *Audubon*, May/June, 1965.

Newman, L. Hugh. "Churchill's Interest in Animal Life." *Audubon*, July/August, 1965.

Newman, L. Hugh. *Living With Butterflies*. London: John Baker, 1967.

136

Newman, L. Hugh, with Savonius, Moira. *Create a Butterfly Garden.* London: John Baker, 1967.

Newsom-Brighton, Maryanne. "Butterflies are Free." *National Wildlife,* April/May, 1982.

Newsom-Brighton, Maryanne. "A Garden of Butterflies." *Organic Gardening,* January, 1983.

Norsgaard, E. Jaediker. "The Lawn That Went Wild." *Ranger Rick's Nature Magazine,* May/June, 1976.

Oates, Matthew. *Garden Plants for Butterflies.* Fareham, Hampshire: Brian Masterson & Associates Limited, 1985.

Oppewall, Jeannine. "History of Butterfly Farming in California." *Terra* 17/4 (1979):30–35.

Owen, Denis F. "Conservation of Butterflies in Garden Habitats." *Environmental Conservation* 3/4 (1976):285–290.

Owen, Denis F. "Insect Diversity in an English Suburban Garden." In *Perspectives in Urban Entomology.* New York: Academic Press, 1978.

Owen, D.F. "Species Diversity in Butterflies in a Tropical Garden." *Biological Conservation* 3/3 (1971):191–198.

Owen, D.F. "Estimating the Abundance and Diversity of Butterflies." *Biological Conservation* 8 (1975):173–183.

Owen, Jennifer, and Owen, D.F. "Suburban Gardens: England's Most Important Nature Reserve?"*Environmental Conservation* 2/1 (1975):53–59.

Peattie, Donald Culross. "How to Attract Butterflies to Your Garden." *Better Homes & Gardens,* August, 1941.

Pyle, Robert Michael. "Railways and Butterflies." *Xerces Society Self-Help Sheet* No. 2, 1974.

Pyle, Robert Michael. "Create a Community Butterfly Reserve." *Xerces Society Self-Help Sheet* No. 4, 1975.

Pyle, Robert Michael. "Butterfly Gardening." In *The Audubon Society Handbook for Butterfly Watchers.* New York: Charles Scribner's Sons, 1984.

*Ranger Rick's Nature Magazine.* "Butterfly Garden." May, 1977.

Reinhard, Harriet V. "Food Plants for Butterflies." California Native Plant Society *Newsletter* 6/4 (1970):3–6.

Rothschild, Miriam and Farrell, Clive. *The Butterfly Gardener.* London: Michael Joseph/Rainbird, 1983.

Simon, Seymour. "Butterflies and Moths." In *Pets in a Jar: Collecting and Caring For Small Wild Animals.* New York: Penguin Books, 1979.

Smith, Alice Upham. "Attracting Butterflies To the Garden." *Horticulture,* August, 1975.

Smith, Jack. "A Passion For Butterflies." *Los Angeles Times, View,* April 13, 1976.

*Smithsonian Magazine,* February, 1979. "She Raises Monarchs in Mid-Manhattan."

Stokes, Bruce. "The Urban Garden: A Growing Trend." *Sierra,* July/August, 1978.

Stone, John L.S. and Midwinter, H.J. *Butterfly Culture: A Guide to Breeding Butterflies, Moths, and Other Insects.* Poole, Dorset, U.K.: Blandford Press, 1975.

*Sunset Magazine,* "They Like Only Passion Vines." April, 1961.

*Sunset Joy of Gardening 1978.* "Attracting Butterflies to Your Garden."

Teale, Edwin Way. *Near Horizons: The Story of An Insect Garden.* London: Robert Hale Limited, 1947.

Tekulsky, Mathew. "Butterfly Gardening." *Family Circle Great Ideas,* February, 1983.

Thomas, Jack Ward; Brush, Robert O.; and DeGraaf, Richard M. "Invite Wildlife To Your Backyard." *National Wildlife,* April-May, 1973. (Available as an updated reprint from the National Wildlife Federation, 1412 Sixteenth Street, N.W., Washington, D.C. 20036.)

Titlow, Debby Igleheart. "Gardens On the Wing." *Colorado Homes & Lifestyles.* May/June, 1984.

Tylka, David. "Butterfly Gardens." *Missouri Conservationist,* June, 1980.

U.S. Department of the Interior. *Estab-

*lishing Trails on Rights-of-Way: Principally Railroad Abandonments.* Superintendent of Documents, U.S. Government Printing Office, Washington, D.C.

Vietmeyer, Noel D. "Butterfly Ranching is Taking Wing in Papua New Guinea." *Smithsonian,* May, 1979.

Vietmeyer, Noel D. (ed.) *Butterfly Farming in Papua New Guinea.* Washington, D.C.: National Academy Press, 1983.

Villiard, Paul. *Moths and How to Rear Them.* New York: Funk & Wagnalls, 1969.

Weaver, Mary Anne. "Barely a Flutter At the World's First Walk-through Butterfly Zoo." *The Christian Science Monitor,* February 22, 1985:11.

Williams, Ted. "A Butterfly Garden." *Garden,* July/August, 1980.

Williams, Ted. "How to Plant a Butterfly Garden." *Sanctuary,* April, 1984.

Wiltshire, Lilas. "Informal Garden Helps Lure Butterflies." *Los Angeles Times,* June 8, 1984, Section 1-A:6.

Wolf, Nancy and Guttentag, Roger. "Butterfly Season." *Eco-News,* May, 1975.

Yajima, Minoru. "The Insectarium at Tama Zoo, Tokyo." *International Zoo Yearbook* 12 (1972):96.

Xerces Society. "Butterfly Gardening—One Way to Increase Urban Wildlife (California Edition)" *Xerces Society Educational Leaflet,* 1978, No. 2.

## Flowers and Gardening

Baker, Herbert G. and Irene. "Some Anthecological Aspects of the Evolution of Nectar-producing Flowers, Particularly Amino Acid Production in Nectar." In *Taxonomy and Ecology.* London: Academic Press, 1973.

Baker, Herbert G. and Hurd, Paul D., Jr. "Intrafloral Ecology." *Annual Review of Entomology* 13(1968):385-414.

Brockman, C. Frank. *Trees of North America.* New York: Golden Press, 1968.

Bruce, Hal. *How to Grow Wildflowers and Wild Shrubs and Trees in Your Own Garden.* New York: Alfred A. Knopf, 1976.

Craighead, John J.; Craighead, Frank C., Jr.; and Davis, Ray J. *A Field Guide to Rocky Mountain Wildflowers.* Boston: Houghton Mifflin, 1963.

Crockett, James Underwood. *Annuals.* New York: Time-Life Books, 1973.

Crockett, James Underwood. *Perennials.* New York: Time-Life Books, 1973.

Crockett, James Underwood and Allen, Oliver E. *Wildflower Gardening.* Alexandria, VA: Time-Life Books, 1977.

Dana, Mrs. William Starr. *How to Know the Wild Flowers.* Revised and edited by Clarence J. Hylander. New York: Dover Publications, 1963. (Originally published New York: Charles Scribner's Sons, 1900.)

Faegri, K. and Pijl, L. van der. *The Principles of Pollination Ecology.* Oxford: Pergamon Press, 1979.

Grant, Verne and Karen A. *Flower Pollination in the Phlox Family.* New York: Columbia University Press, 1965.

Headstrom, Richard. *Suburban Wildflowers: An Introduction to the Common Wildflowers of Your Back Yard and Local Park.* Englewood Cliffs, NJ: Prentice-Hall, 1984.

Hersey, Jean. *The Woman's Day Book of Wildflowers.* New York: Simon and Schuster, 1976.

Hull, Helen S. *Wild Flowers for Your Garden.* New York: Gramercy Publishing Company, 1952.

Kevan, Peter G. "Pollination and Environmental Conservation." *Environmental Conservation* 2/4 (1975):293-98.

Knuth, Dr. Paul. *Handbook of Flower Pollination: Based Upon Hermann Muller's Work 'The Fertilisation of Flowers by Insects.'* (Volume 1: Introduction and Literature). Oxford: The Clarendon Press, 1906.

Kruckeberg, Arthur R. *Gardening with Native Plants of the Pacific Northwest.* Seattle: University of Washington Press, 1982.

Lacy, Allen. "Butterfly Weed." In *Home Ground: A Gardener's Miscellany.* New York: Farrar, Straus and Giroux, 1984.

Mecuse, Bastiaan and Morris, Sean. *The Sex Life of Flowers*. New York: Facts on File.

Muller, Hermann. *The Fertilisation of Flowers*. London: Macmillan and Co., 1883.

Niehaus, Theodore F. *A Field Guide to Pacific States Wildflowers*. Boston: Houghton Mifflin, 1976.

Niering, William A. and Olmstead, Nancy C. *The Audubon Society Field Guide to North American Wildflowers: Eastern Region*. New York: Alfred A. Knopf, 1979.

Peterson, Roger Tory and McKenny, Margaret. *A Field Guide to Wildflowers of Northeastern and North-central North America*. Boston: Houghton Mifflin, 1968.

Proctor, Michael and Yeo, Peter. *The Pollination of Flowers*. London: Collins, 1973.

Ray, Mary Helen and Nicholls, Robert P., eds. *A Guide to Significant & Historic Gardens of America*. Athens, GA: Agee Publishers, 1983.

Richards, A.J., ed. *The Pollination of Flowers by Insects*. London and Orlando, Fl.: Academic Press, Linnean Society Symposium Series No. 6, 1978.

Ruggiero, Michael A. *Spotter's Guide to Wild Flowers of North America*. New York: Mayflower Books, 1979.

Sinnes, A. Cort. *All About Annuals*. San Francisco: Ortho Books, 1981.

Sinnes, A. Cort. *All About Perennials*. San Francisco: Ortho Books, 1981.

Spellenberg, Richard. *The Audubon Society Field Guide to North American Wildflowers: Western Region*. New York: Alfred A. Knopf, 1979.

Spencer, Edwin Rollin. *All About Weeds*. New York: Dover Publications, 1974.

Sperka, Marie. *Growing Wildflowers: A Gardener's Guide*. New York: Charles Scribner's Sons, 1984.

Steffek, Edwin F. *The New Wild Flowers and How to Grow Them*. Beaverton, OR: Timber Press, 1983.

Sunset Books. *Color in Your Garden*. Menlo Park, CA: Lane Publishing Co., 1975.

Sunset Books. *Sunset New Western Garden Book*. Menlo Park, CA: Lane Publishing Co., 1984.

Taylor, Kathryn S. and Hamblin, Stephen F. *Handbook of Wild Flower Cultivation*. New York: The Macmillan Company, 1963.

Tenenbaum, Frances. *Gardening with Wild Flowers*. New York: Charles Scribner's Sons, 1973.

United States Department of Agriculture. *Common Weeds of the United States*. New York: Dover Publications, 1971.

Zim, Herbert S. and Martin, Alexander C. *Flowers*. New York: Golden Press, 1950.

# INDEX

# FIELD NOTES

# FIELD NOTES

# FIELD NOTES